(38)

Edward Rowe Snow

True Tales of Terrible Shipwrecks

Also by Edward Rowe Snow

Women of the Sea
Mysterious Tales of the New England Coast
New England Sea Tragedies
Piracy, Mutiny and Murder
Great Sea Rescues and Tales of Survival
Legends of the New England Coast
The Vengeful Sea
Famous Lighthouses of America
Amazing Sea Stories Never Told Before
True Tales of Pirates and Their Gold
Great Gales and Dire Disasters
True Tales of Buried Treasure

TRUE TALES
of Terrible Shipwrecks

BY EDWARD ROWE SNOW

ILLUSTRATED

⚓

DODD, MEAD & COMPANY, NEW YORK

To
Thomas Johnson
whose lasting friendship through
childhood and manhood has been an
inspiration

Introduction

⚓

This volume is the third in a series of True Tales which I have written. I have attempted to put myself in the place of readers who are interested in the sea and to include those stories which a youth or older person who had never been near the sea would find most entertaining. I have chosen shipwrecks which have occurred from time to time along the shore or in the depths of the ocean, and in the first part of this book have told of several craft which went down with treasure aboard.

At this time I wish to show my appreciation for those of you who have read the first two books of this series. *True Tales of Buried Treasure* is now in its tenth printing and *True Tales of Pirates and Their Gold* has been reprinted for the sixth time.

A perfect setting for reading this volume would be somewhere along the coast when wintry gales are stirring up the mighty ocean and the surf is thundering with awesome fury against the shores. At the very height of this terrible tempest, I suggest that you sit down and relax in your comfortable chair in front of a roaring, crackling fire, and begin reading the first chapter of this book.

More than 16,600 wrecks and almost 580 storms were studied before I chose the chapters which have been included, and I trust that my variety of choice meets with the approval of the reader.

I shall never forget the kindness of those who assisted me in the writing of this volume, and several who helped considerably have not allowed me to mention them here. Alice Powers Blackington, Alton Hall Blackington, Mary E. Brown, Avis G. Clarke, Walter S. Ehrenfeld, Margaret Hackett, Marie Hansen, Melina Herron, Laurence P. Macdonald, William F. McIntire, Muriel A. McKenzie, Foster L. Palmer, Ethel M. Ritchie, Lawrence H. Rideout, Joan Spunt, Mrs. James E. Sumner, Sandra Undergraves, Howard White and Barbara Whitledge.

Mr. John R. Herbert, Editor of *The Patriot Ledger* of Quincy, Massachusetts, on several occasions made it possible for me to obtain needed material for this book.

My wife Anna-Myrle spent many hours on reading the galley sheets to prevent me from falling into any errors, but the accuracy of all statements in the text is my responsibility alone.

Edward Rowe Snow

Contents

⚓

PART I: TREASURE IN THE SEA

ONE Treasure in Boston Bay 3

TWO The Circus Ship and Its Treasure 9

THREE The Treasure Ship *Central America* 19

PART II: WRECKS IN NEW ENGLAND WATERS

FOUR The *Watch and Wait* 31

FIVE The Immigrant Ship *Saint John* 37

SIX The *City of Columbus* 43

SEVEN The Steamer *Portland* 50

EIGHT The Monomoy Disaster 65

NINE The *Larchmont* Disaster 70

PART III: WRECKS IN ATLANTIC WATERS

TEN The *Phoenix* 79

ELEVEN The *Atalante* 91

(ix)

TWELVE Loss of the Indiaman *Kent* 97

THIRTEEN Eaten by Sharks 103

FOURTEEN Collins, the Good Samaritan 113

FIFTEEN Arctic Adventure 121

SIXTEEN The *Monitor* 130

PART IV: WRECKS IN AFRICAN AND ASIAN WATERS

SEVENTEEN The Castaways of the *Doddington* 147

EIGHTEEN A Frenchman's Adventure in India 156

NINETEEN The Whitmonday Wreck 164

TWENTY The *Winterton*'s Castaways 170

TWENTY-ONE The *Fanny* in the Chinese Ocean 175

PART V: WRECKS IN EUROPEAN WATERS

TWENTY-TWO *Mary Rose, Vasa* and *Royal George* 187

TWENTY-THREE The *Ajax* 202

TWENTY-FOUR The Steamer *Killarney* 208

TWENTY-FIVE The Strange Voyage of the *Vryheid* 214

APPENDIX: Latitude and Longitude of Craft Which Went Down in the Massachusetts Bay Area 225

GLOSSARY 227

INDEX 231

Illustrations

Following page 84

Wreck of Captain Morton's ship on Shag Rocks
Bone of elephant drowned on the *Royal Tar*
Sinking of the *Central America*
Wreck of the *Watch and Wait*
Loss of the *Phoenix*
The *Kent* destroyed by fire
Survivors of the *Kent*
Doddington wrecked off South Africa
Survivors of the *Doddington*
Shipwreck of the *Jonge Thomas*
Castaways from the *Winterton*
The *Fanny* wrecked off China
Sinking of the *Royal George*
Removing wreckage of the *Royal George*
The *Killarney* wrecked off the Irish coast
Survivors of the *Vryheid* wreck

PART I

TREASURE IN THE SEA

⚓

CHAPTER ONE

Treasure in Boston Bay

A fortune estimated at between $1,866,000,000 and $2,117,-000,000 in gold, silver and other metals and still-usable cargo material has gone to the bottom off the coasts of Europe, Africa and the Americas since the beginning of recorded history, and more of it can be salvaged today than the average reader appreciates.

Off the New England shores alone treasure valued probably in excess of $687,000,000 could theoretically be brought to the surface, but to do it, a type of man who has not been much in evidence around Massachusetts since the days of the clipper ships is needed.

More than a score of treasure chests have gone to the sea bottom within fourteen miles of the Boston, Massachusetts, Lightship, many of them in the depths of Boston Bay. Their total value might run as high as $3,000,000. Strangely enough, the oldest known treasure ship sunk in the area contains bars of silver which are believed to have been seen by a resident of Quincy, Massachusetts, as recently as in 1960. The search for another treasure, this one pieces of eight, has brought to light only the vessel's anchor, which was discovered near Shag Rocks off Boston Light. Among other valuable wrecks, one is said to contain more than 19,000 of the famous 1804 silver dollars; and the *City of Salisbury,* loaded with a cargo worth an estimated $1,500,000, hit uncharted rocks near Graves Ledge.*

Late in the night of November 27, 1682, a silver ship approached the islands of Boston Harbor in a blinding southeasterly snowstorm. The thirteen men aboard had lost all sense of direction, and three of them went out on deck to attempt to identify some landmark. Suddenly a gigantic wave hit the craft and heeled her over. When the decks cleared, the others saw that the three had been washed overboard to their death.

A moment later the vessel shattered on a rocky ledge, but not before the remaining ten men clambered hastily aboard their shallop. Carried by the wind and the waves, the survivors were thrown ashore on a sandy beach about two hours later.

Having no idea where they were, they began hiking through the deep drifts, and soon the weaker ones began to drop from exhaustion. Finally, far in the distance they could see a light, but four of them never lived to reach that haven, freezing to death one by one in the heavy drifts.

The remaining six men were guided by the light to the home of Deane Winthrop, son of John Winthrop, whose house was in what is now the town of Winthrop between the

---

* Other craft whose strong boxes or treasure chests are still on the bottom of Boston Bay include the *Kadosh, Tedesco, Exile, Elizabeth and Ann, Maritana, Joachim, Ewan Crewar, Allentown, Vernon* and *Hazard.*

present Terrace Avenue and Shirley Street.* Deane Winthrop
did all he could for the unfortunate guests, who recovered
their health to leave for their homes.

The great cargo of silver, although hunted on many occasions, has never been discovered. In 1960 scuba † diver
Charles Wood, of Quincy, was exploring the underwater
area in about thirty-five feet of water. Swimming along close
to the bottom, he noticed amongst the wreckage of an ancient
craft a score or more of what he thought might be ballast
stones. The stones were arranged in what probably once had
been orderly rows. Scratching at several of the loaf-shaped
objects, he scraped off the barnacles and sea growth.

High overhead, the sun and the clouds were playing hide
and seek. When sunlight occasionally filtered down through
the water it revealed a silverish gleam which mystified him.
It looked like silver but it seemed that it could not be, for
he knew of no Spanish galleons having been lost in the area.
That night, however, he began wondering about his experience, and later told me of it.

"Did you take careful bearings of the location?" I asked.

"Not careful, but I can find the spot, or within fifty feet
of it."

"Well," I explained, "you have probably discovered the
legendary silver ship lost in Boston Bay in 1682. Every one
of those silver bars, if they are silver bars, may be worth
eighteen hundred dollars!"

Charlie Wood has returned to the general location on several occasions, but—and perhaps you have guessed it—so far
he has not located the 280-year-old treasure of the silver ship
of Boston Bay.

On the night of December 4, 1768, Captain Thomas Mor-

---

* A marker identifies the location today.
† Self-contained underwater breathing apparatus.

ton was bringing his brig loaded with sugar and molasses into Boston Harbor when the vessel struck heavily on Shag Rocks, off the shores of Boston Light.

A substantial treasure chest filled with pieces of eight was lost with Captain Morton's vessel, which went to pieces almost at once. The master told representatives of the local Boston newspaper, and the disappearance of the great treasure chest was duly recorded in the next issue of the journal.

Down through the years Captain Morton's pieces of eight have been the object of many treasure hunts, but so far nothing but the anchor from the brig has ever been recovered.

Thirty-six years later, in 1804, the government mint at Washington produced 19,570 silver dollars. The following year only 321 were minted, and after that, thirty years went by without another issue of the coin.

After a few of the 1804 dollars had been set aside, and some say the number is less than twenty, the remainder were carefully boxed and prepared for shipment.

The tradition in some numismatic circles is that the coins were put aboard a vessel whose destination was Boston, and that she had an uneventful voyage until reaching Massachusetts Bay, where she encountered a wild hurricane. Legend has it that she went down not far from Boston Light.

When it is realized that the last time one of the 1804 silver dollars was sold it brought the sum of $29,000, possibly some ambitious scuba diver may begin active research to separate legend from fact. Nineteen thousand silver dollars of the year 1804 might bring a substantial amount. Multiplying 19,000 by $29,000 approaches the somewhat astronomical figure of $551,000,000. Of course the catch is that the more 1804 silver dollars which are known to exist by the general public the smaller the relative value of each coin.

* * *

Entering Boston Harbor on April 22, 1938, in a dense fog, the heavily laden 419-foot cargo steamer *City of Salisbury*, with Captain Owen Morris as master, struck an uncharted pinnacle twenty-four feet below the surface and was unable to move. Loaded with animals, rubber, jute and many other supplies, the *Salisbury* contained the richest cargo ever wrecked in outer Boston Harbor. The cargo was valued at $1,500,000. I was lucky enough to make the first air photograph of the disaster later that April afternoon when we found a rift in the thick fog bank and dropped down through. It was a thrill to circle above the huge vessel and to see the animal crates, the Lascars with their life belts on, and the general state of orderly excitement on the steamer as the vessel slowly settled upon the ledge.

Barges began to unload the steamer, but it was too late. Shortly after noon the next day an ominous sound was heard, and the vessel cracked in two. The many animals aboard were hurriedly brought into Boston, with the exception of two snakes and several monkeys which disappeared in the confusion. One of the monkeys appeared later in the week five miles away on Deer Island, where he was seen by Robert Mackey, of Point Shirley, while Nelson Maynard, of Deer Island, found the carcass of a large snake on the same beach.

All the following summer the *City of Salisbury* hung on the pinnacle, with much of the cargo removed by the last of August. Excursion steamers took thousands upon thousands of people out by the wreck, for it was a spectacular sight. The steamer was rechristened "Zoo Ship" by those who saw her grinding away on the ledge that year. By midsummer the entire forward section had slipped off into deep water, and a crack was developing amidships of the remainder of the vessel. When the autumn winds began to blow, the stern alone was above the water. It was a weird sensation to the writer and others who went aboard the afterdeck two weeks before she sank completely. The grinding and gnashing of the iron rods and broken timbers far down under the water could plainly be heard, and the steamer would shudder and jerk as the ground swell passed alongside. She survived the great New England hurricane of September 21, 1938, which caused the death of 682 persons and damage in the hundreds of millions, but a northeasterly storm during October came in out of the Atlantic, and when it had cleared, the *City of Salisbury* was no longer visible.

Material was still being removed from the hold by divers as late as 1962. Although all the crew were saved, there was one fatality connected with the disaster. A Medford mechanic, William J. Satovan, forty-two, drowned when he was lost overboard on his trip to the wreck as a sightseer in a small boat.

The pilot aboard the *City of Salisbury*, Captain William H. Lewis, of Wollaston, knew that his course had been an accurate one, and was exonerated of any blame in the shipwreck when it was found that Government Chart 246 was incorrect.

His story follows: "I reported that the rock was uncharted and the Coast Guard investigated and reported also that the chart was wrong. The chart at that point gave us thirty-three feet of water, and with the draft of the vessel, we should have cleared it easily."

The rock on which the *Salisbury* cracked apart was later named Salisbury Pinnacle. All coastal surveys had missed it since earliest times because the soundings had taken place all around the pinnacle, unfortunately never hitting it.

Out on the great ship, cargo originally worth more than $400,000 is still aboard the *City of Salisbury*, but, of course, only a small proportion of that amount will ever be realized even if the goods are salvaged.

CHAPTER TWO

The Circus Ship and Its Treasure

On the sea bottom in Penobscot Bay, Maine, not far from Vinalhaven, lies a treasure chest loaded with gold and silver coins. It has been there since the year 1836. If certain plans now being made concerning that treasure are successfully carried out, the money chest may be brought into Biddeford, Maine, within the relatively near future. What the condition of the gold and silver will be after an immersion of more than a century and a quarter has caused much discussion in the scuba diving fraternity. Inside the chest are the entire receipts of the successful touring season of a circus known as the Dexter's Locomotive Museum and Burgess' Collection of Serpents and Birds, collected in New Brunswick that year of 1836.

The troupe was being transported aboard the steamer *Royal Tar,* named for King William IV of England, which was 164 feet long and had been built that spring at Saint

John. The circus was so large that it was necessary to remove and leave behind several of the lifeboats from the hurricane deck of the vessel to make room for the equipment to be stored there. The treasure chest was placed in the purser's quarters, and the animals were brought aboard. The menagerie included Mogul the elephant, two pelicans, two camels, several horses, a Royal Bengal tiger, a gnu and many other animals and birds. After the *Royal Tar* was loaded, she sailed from Saint John on October 21, 1836, bound for Portland, Maine.

Soon reaching the open sea, the steamer proceeded south. At first the water was perfect in every respect, but before the sun went down that Friday a high westerly wind began to blow. Continuing for several days the gale eventually forced the side-wheeler to seek shelter in Eastport Harbor, and there she remained until Tuesday.

Leaving Eastport Harbor Tuesday afternoon, the *Royal Tar* was again hit by rising winds. For a second time she sought shelter, this time finding a lee behind Fox Island in Penobscot Bay. Then, while she was anchored two miles off Fox Island Thoroughfare, orders were given to fill her boilers.

Pilot Atkins' son, attracted by the intense blistering heat of the wooden beams near the boilers, tested the lower cock only to find it dry. He told his father, who mentioned the fact to Second Engineer Marshall, then in charge. In no uncertain language the boy and father were made to understand that they were greatly mistaken in thinking that the boilers were dry. They were told by the indignant Mr. Marshall, "Everything is in perfect order!"

Actually, as was later discovered, the regular engineer had been up working all night on the boilers. He had retired to his bunk, giving the task of filling the boilers to his second engineer, who in turn had ordered the fireman to do this important job, but the fireman had failed to carry out the command.

A few seconds after the discussion the boilers became red hot, setting fire to two wedges which had been inserted between them and the elephant cage. The flames soon spread, and the crew quickly organized to fight the fire.

In the cabin, the passengers were about to sit down to dinner when they heard a strange commotion outside. Captain Reed, rushing to the companionway, took one look at the flames leaping up through the grating and realized that the *Royal Tar* was doomed. It was then blowing a gale offshore. The foresail caught fire immediately, and the jib, which was raised, was burned through almost at once.

"Slip the anchor," the captain shouted, "and hoist a distress signal."

Captain Reed realized with sinking heart that the two lifeboats left behind in Saint John were going to be desperately needed. All that remained were the longboat and the jolly boat, both of which he ordered launched.

Many persons jumped into the longboat. The crew cut the ropes to drop the craft into the water and soon were rowing away from the blazing steamer toward the distant shore. Captain Reed leaped into the jolly boat to prevent its being taken away. About twenty men still on the *Royal Tar* tried to tip overboard one of the great omnibuses which on land were used to transport the circus, but in this they failed.

A short time later the revenue cutter *Veto*, stationed at Castine, was sighted five miles away. As she drew near, Reed had a few survivors get into the jolly boat, after which he rowed them across to the *Veto*. Learning that the cutter was shorthanded and without her regular commanding officer, Captain Reed volunteered to take the wheel briefly and explain to the helmsman what should be done. He also planned to send some of his own men over to help out the sailors on the cutter. Since she had a load of powder aboard she could not sail too close to the burning steamer, then drifting help-lessly out to sea.

By staying far enough away from the *Royal Tar*, Captain Reed prevented the panic-stricken survivors from leaping into and swamping his boat. One by one he ordered the desperate passengers to jump into the water and grab his oar, and then he pulled them into the jolly boat. In this way he was able to transport a total of almost fifty persons from the *Royal Tar* to the *Veto*.

Some of the experiences both survivors and victims under-went were heart-rending. The *Veto*'s gig was launched under the command of the pilot, who was afraid to get too close to the flames. Passing around to the stern, he noticed many pas-sengers who could not swim hanging to ropes put over the side of the burning craft. When they shouted to him for help he lost his nerve completely, ordering the gig back to the cutter. Soon afterward the flames reached the ropes, burned through and dropped the unfortunate victims into the water to their doom. If the pilot had not lost his head, more than twenty of those who died in this way would have been saved.

Feeling that otherwise they would perish, a group of men then began putting together a makeshift float which they managed to get over the side and into the sea. Just as they were clambering down onto the raft there was a terrific blast of hot air and burning embers from the blaze, followed almost at once by the sound of the frenzied elephant, Mogul, trumpeting in terror.

At the very moment that the men were aboard their raft and about to push off, the creature appeared immediately above them. Placing his forepaws on the taffrail as he was ac-customed to do during a trick he performed in the circus, the huge beast smashed through the rail. Carrying several desperate humans with him, he hurtled down on the raft and its occupants, submerging the men forever in the sea.

Minutes later the elephant was seen coming to the surface, after which he started to swim for the nearest land, but as the *Royal Tar* was then more than five miles out to sea, Mogul evidently perished before he reached shore. His lifeless body was found floating a few days later near Brimstone Island.*

Aboard the ship were six horses whose duty it had been to pull the huge locomotive museum. They were released and backed into the ocean, after which three of them swam instinctively for the nearest land and were saved, while the other three circled the burning craft until they became exhausted and sank beneath the waves.

One passenger, who had carried aboard ship a large number of silver coins, decided to fasten his money belt around his waist with five hundred dollars in silver in it. Since he was a good swimmer he had no fear when he mounted the taffrail and leaped into the sea, but he had forgotten the heavy weight of the coins. He never came to the surface, dragged down by his wealth to his doom in the waters of Penobscot Bay. The treasure chest was never given a thought in the frantic efforts each person made to save his own life.

Mr. H. H. Fuller, one of the officials in the circus, told of how he had been seasick in his berth when the fire broke out:

When I reached the deck I saw the longboat full of people, a quarter of a mile to leeward; they were rowing hard and soon out of sight. The small boat, in which was Captain Reed, who took possession of it to prevent its following the longboat to the leeward, lay about fifty yards astern; three persons swam

---

* Mr. Roy Coombs, of Vinalhaven, preserved a fragment of the huge skeleton for many years. In 1944 I received in the mail from a member of the Coombs family the skeletal remains of Mogul's foot.

off, and were taken into her, though the wind was then blowing a gale, and a tremendous sea was running. He then bore away for the land, to the windward about two miles. At this time a great many persons jumped overboard and were drowned. The screams of the women and children, the horrid yells of the men, the roaring of the storm, and the awful confusion, baffle description. . . . The steamer then broached to and was shortly afterward completely enveloped in flames amidships. The fire interrupted all communication fore and aft; and neither those in the bow nor those in the stern could see or know the fate of each other. All but myself fled from the quarter-deck. I sat on the stern rail, till my coat caught fire. I looked round, and seeing not a soul . . . fastened a rope to the tiller chain and dropped over the stern, where I found about fifteen others hanging in various places, most in the water.

As Mr. Fuller hung there, he saw several of the survivors drop off to their death, but he had fastened his rope to the chain, which was in turn fastened to iron bolts, and Fuller knew that the iron would not catch fire. He took a turn with the line around his "neck and thigh," and in this manner was able to bear the weight of four others, three men and a lady, "who hung securely to me."

A thrilling drama was enacted a short distance from Fuller. Pilot Atkins was holding a woman with his feet when her strength finally failed and she began to slip from his grasp. He let himself down a short distance and was able to grasp her again with his feet, holding her in the water against the ship. Then a terrific wave smashed against them, and she was washed away. For a minute it seemed as if she were lost. Miraculously the next wave dashed her against another man, to whom she clung desperately.

At that moment the cutter's gig passed close by, but although pitiful entreaties were directed at its pilot, the gig went away without helping anyone. Finally Captain Reed came in and rescued her and the other survivors around the tiller, taking them across to the cutter.

William Marjoram, a deck passenger, remembered that while passing the cage of the lion on deck he thought of the psalmist David who said, "My soul is among lions, even those that are set on fire." He was encouraged when he noticed the cutter approaching, but his heart sank when she began to sail away. Later, however, he saw Captain Reed board her with some of his sailors to man her, and then the captain began ferrying passengers across from the burning *Royal Tar* to the *Veto*.

Marjoram's story follows:

I was three hours on the wreck, and was taken off by the Captain. The moment I got on board of the cutter, I begged Captain Dyer to carry her alongside, but he refused; saying the elephant would jump board. I then requested him to sail the cutter under the bows, and ask the keeper to lash his (the elephant's) leg to the windlass; but it was of no avail; he ordered me to go below, which I did for a short time. I again went on deck, and helped the people out of the boat as they came alongside, remarking every time that they brought no women with them.

About six o'clock the boat came with only three persons on board—a Mr. Brown, late steward of the boat, and a colored sailor, that belonged to the steamboat, who was the means of saving a great many lives, having been in the boat a long time. He requested me to take his place, the cutter-master said he could stay no longer.

I . . . jumped into the boat and rowed away; on reaching the wreck there was one woman holding on the bowsprit, with a child in her arms, and another in the water, with her clothes burnt off, holding on by a piece of rope; she let go, and before I could get to her the child was drowned; but we saved the woman, who was nearly dead. . . . The cutter stood from the shore, where she landed the survivors, except the last woman; Captain Dyer and myself sitting up all night, endeavoring to bring her to, which we did.

The shore mentioned by Marjoram was Isle au Haut, where the revenue cutter *Veto* had taken the survivors. The inhabitants on the island cared for their needs.

Another passenger, Stimson Patten, of Saint John, New Brunswick, was warm in praise of Captain Reed, saying that "to him all credit is due for his deliberate and manly perseverance throughout the whole calamity. It is impossible to describe the appalling spectacle which the whole scene presented—the boat wrapped in flames, with nearly 100 souls on board, without any hope of relief, rending the air with their shrieks for help; the caravan of wild beasts on deck, ready to tear to pieces all that might escape the flames."

Shortly before sunset the last rescue boat with a single survivor left the *Royal Tar*. Still blazing fiercely, the side-wheeler continued to drift out to sea, and the light of the conflagration was still visible at seven in the evening, after which it suddenly disappeared. The steamer is believed to have gone down into the sea at that moment about twenty miles from the place where she had taken fire seven hours earlier.

Captain Reed was soon subjected to the usual criticism a sea captain faces after a disaster, but he came out of the ordeal with flying colors. As mentioned above, when the revenue cutter arrived on the scene she was undermanned and in the charge of a Lieutenant Dyer, who was uncertain of what to do. With a cargo of powder aboard, which he could easily have dumped into the sea to leeward, Dyer was afraid to approach too near, and so Captain Reed put his own crew aboard and personally supervised the ferry service. More lives would have been saved if the man in command of the gig had not been afraid. But when everything is taken into consideration, the proportion of survivors was high. Thirty-two people perished, and only one person burned to death in the flames, an old lady who did not appear on deck at all. Of the ninety-three persons aboard, sixty-one, or almost two-thirds, were eventually saved. Most of the others lost their lives by leaping into the sea in panic or slipping to their death in the ocean when the ropes to which they were clinging burned through.

On October 26, 1836, while ashore at Isle au Haut, Captain Reed wrote a letter to Leonard Billings, steamboat agent at Portland. Part of his statement follows:

"I have no blame to attach to anyone—I think that it was pure accident. I am very stiffened from overexertion, but hope to be better shortly. The people here have been very kind, indeed, and we are as well off as can be expected."

The passengers at Isle au Haut obtained a schooner to take them to Portland, while the master and crew later returned to Eastport on another craft.

Captain Thomas Reed was highly regarded for the remainder of his life for his outstanding bravery during the burning of the *Royal Tar*. On November 3, 1836, he was presented with a purse of $699 for his heroism during the fire. Later he was appointed harbormaster of Saint John, where for many years he was a picturesque figure along the water front and was often seen walking from wharf to wharf with his faithful dog at his side.

Whenever a group of boys would visit him, he would tell the tale of the loss of his beautiful side-wheeler. One of his favorite stories became the account of the great treasure chest, bulging with gold and silver, which still lay at the bottom of the sea in the bowels of the *Royal Tar*. Possibly inspired by his stories, several adventurers left Saint John shortly after the middle of the last century to explore the bottom for the wreck of the ship and the treasure chest. They found neither. My cousin, the late Willis Snow, genealogical wizard of the Snow family, once kept the lighthouse in the Fox Island Thoroughfare. During his free time he made several trips to the scenes of the wreck of the man-of-war *Albany* and the *Royal Tar*. One very calm day he looked down through the clear water to sight several of the guns of the *Albany* on the Triangle Ledges, but he never did find the hull of the *Royal Tar*.

Judging from all reports, there may be about $35,000 in the treasure chest aboard the sunken side-wheeler. Many new methods of bringing up sunken treasure have been invented recently, and one man claims that he can locate coins at the sea bottom forty feet down! Possibly before this present generation ends the coins from the *Royal Tar* may be brought to the surface.

CHAPTER THREE

The Treasure Ship *Central America*

⚓

The greatest amount of treasure from sunken ships ever recovered off the shores of North America was $1,250,000 in gold and silver brought to the surface in 1687 by Maine-born Sir William Phips. This vast hoard came from a Spanish galleon which had gone down forty-six years earlier * off the coast of Hispaniola.

Nevertheless, it is entirely within the realm of possibility, because of almost unbelievable strides forward in undersea detection, that a substantially larger treasure may be brought to the surface off the shores of Cape Hatteras from the wreck of the ill-fated *Central America*.† In 1857 this proud packet ship sank with $2,345,000 in gold which is still on the bottom of the sea off North Carolina.

Why is there so much gold aboard the ship? The answer is

* See my *True Tales of Buried Treasure*, pages 1–19.
† Originally named the *George Law*.

a fairly simple one. Not only was there a great gold shipment in the strongbox of the *Central America,* but that same purser's room held another treasure chest which was literally bulging with sacks of gold dust, fifty-dollar gold pieces and the rare Sacramento ingots:

```
F. D. KOHLER
    STATE ASSAYER  DW ͭ
CARAT     CAL =   44 3/4
   21 1/8   1850     CTS
                  $40.07
```

The Kohler Ingot, Now Worth $6,000

In addition to the two treasure chests in the purser's quarters there was more than $525,000 aboard still in the possession of scores of grizzled miners and cautious veterans of the gold fields. Each had taken his substantial hoard right into his stateroom with him and kept his fortune close by his side at all times. Several of the miners are believed to have had scores of the rare Sacramento ingots whose value today is said to be from $5,000 to $10,000 each!

By 1857 communication between the Far West and the East had been reduced to three main channels of travel. The average person could go aboard a clipper ship around South America's stormy Cape Horn, cross the United States by pack horse and trails, or sail to the Isthmus of Panama for the short land trip between oceans. Most of the wealthy gold miners usually chose the latter route.

On August 20, 1857, the steamship *Sonora* had left San Francisco in the Pacific with the same passengers and treasure which ultimately sailed aboard the *Central America* in the

Atlantic Ocean. Arriving in Panama, the money and passengers were taken across the Isthmus on Friday, September 1, after which the transfer to the packet ship took place.

The *Central America* sailed from Aspinwall City * on September 3 under Captain W. L. Herndon,† who, at forty-four, carried the rank of commander in the United States Navy. He had assumed this command two years before and had already taken thousands of men and women to fever-ridden Aspinwall City and brought back no less than $32,800,000 in gold.

Reaching Havana on this voyage, the *Central America* unloaded freight and then started for the United States on September 8. There were 101 members of the crew and 474 passengers when she passed beyond Morro Castle.

A gale began that same day, and as the ship proceeded toward New York, the wind increased in intensity. Late Thursday night, the tenth, the straining of the ship's hull was evident to everyone aboard, and by Friday morning the creaking and groaning of the vessel had grown worse. Therefore it was no surprise to Captain Herndon when he was informed that the ship was beginning to leak in the seams amidships, and shortly after this report the water began to pour in by the barrelful. Soon it had filled the entire hold of the ship, and when it reached the boilers there was a terrible hissing sound as the fires went out one by one. With the fires dead, the pumps became useless, and a gigantic bucket brigade was formed. The crew and passengers pitched in with such enthusiasm that they gained on the water for a time, and the fires were rekindled.

Unfortunately, their elation was short-lived, for the water soon began rising once more, and when the fires went out

* Now known as Colon.
† His sister was Ellen Herndon, who had married the great naval scientist, Commander Matthew Fontaine Maury.

this time, it was forever. Bailing continued, hour after hour. Entirely at the mercy of wind and waves, the rolling, pitching ship soon became waterlogged.

By the morning of Saturday, the twelfth, it was apparent to almost everyone that the *Central America* was doomed and that the time of her sinking was within a matter of only hours. Still the bailing went on, however, and the passengers carried out this arduous task without complaint. The storm had now developed into a hurricane with twenty- and thirty-foot waves making up.

At two o'clock on Saturday afternoon all hands were heartened by the lookout, who reported a sail to windward. Within the hour a brig, the *Marine,* out of Boston, her master Captain Burt, came sailing up alongside and passed under the stern of the wallowing ship.

There were five lifeboats on the *Central America,* two of which were now launched into the sea only to be destroyed at once by the waves. Three boats remained, one of which was in poor condition, having been struck by several heavy seas which had swept across the boat deck.

The next launching, at four o'clock in the afternoon, was successful. The boat made a series of successful trips loaded with women and children until all but the men were aboard the *Marine.* By this time there was some distance separating the two craft.

On the next trip the chief engineer and fifteen others started in the lifeboat for the brig. As night descended, the boat did not return after reaching the rescue craft. When the final passenger to be rescued by the lifeboat was about to leave, Captain Herndon had stepped quickly toward him.

"Please give this watch to my wife," * he said. "Tell her from me that I . . ." Herndon could not finish and walked

---

* At home with their family including daughter Ellen, later wife of Chester A. Arthur, twenty-fifth President of the United States.

away. The lifeboat descended into the sea, and made the stormy crossing in the gathering darkness to the *Marine*.

Herndon returned to the bridge of his ship and watched the passengers continue to bail. An hour later, the decks were awash and all bailing stopped. Life preservers were handed around to the passengers, and Captain Herndon told his officers that although he would never leave the ship, they should try to save themselves.

Some time later another ship came along, the *El Dorado*, but her master, Captain Stone, understood Captain Herndon to say that the *Central America* should stay afloat until morning when the *El Dorado* could take off the remaining survivors.

As the night wore on Captain Herndon had the foreyard set down. Trying desperately to get the *Central America* before the wind, he found that no canvas was strong enough to endure the gale then blowing. There was nothing else to do but to cut away the foremast, out of which a crude sea anchor was built and put astern. The water now was approaching the level of the main deck. Fragments of sail were bent on, but in vain, for the *Central America* rolled heavily in the trough of the sea. Suddenly, the vessel gave three violent lurches, listing to an angle of forty-five degrees, and plunged stern first with "every timber quivering" to disappear forever.

A short time before the ship sank, Captain Herndon had told Chief Officer Van Rennselaer that he was going below. A few minutes later the captain reappeared on the bridge, attired in full dress uniform! Removing the oilskin cover that kept his naval cap insignia dry, he stood firm and erect, a striking figure.

When the ship gave a warning lurch, recovering only with greatest difficulty, Herndon asked for volunteers to chop free the pilothouse and make a raft of it. After the *Central America* sank, he and several in the crew could be seen floating on the pilothouse for a time, but soon the others washed off and the captain was alone.

As they drifted away on fragments of the forecastle, the crew watched him trying to keep his balance. Holding his telescope, Herndon waved back to those on the wreckage. His uniformed body was still ramrod straight as the wheelhouse took him into the mist and out of sight forever.

One of the most brilliant naval officers of his time, Herndon had distinguished himself in the war with Mexico. He had been at the Washington Naval Observatory for several years, after which he explored the Amazon River under the direction of the United States government.

On the morning after the sinking, September 13, 1857, the Norwegian bark *Ellen* came running down with a free wind. Wreckage from the *Central America* was sighted, and then the cries of passengers still afloat were heard coming from the broken timbers. At nine o'clock, thirty-one were saved after five hours in the sea.

Many thrilling narratives of their personal sufferings were told by some of the passengers. That of Mr. George furnished an idea of the terrors of a night on the waves. Mr. George was one of the hundreds who had supplied themselves with life preservers, pieces of plank, etc., and preferred to await the ship's going down to leaping overboard in anticipation of her fate. When she sank he was dragged, with the rest on board of her, some twenty-five feet below the surface.

He "heard no shriek—nothing but the seething rush and hiss of waters that closed above her as she hurried, almost with the speed of an arrow, to her ocean bed." He was sucked in by "the whirlpool caused by her swift descent, to a depth that was seemingly unfathomable, and into a darkness that he had never dreamed of. Compared with it, the blackest night, without moon or star, was as broad noonday."

He was stunned rather than stifled, and his sensations on

coming to the surface were almost as painful, in reaction, as those which he endured at the greatest depth to which he sank. When he became conscious, after the lapse of a minute or two, he could distinguish every object around him for a considerable distance. The waves, as they rose and fell, revealed a sea of human heads. Those unfortunates who had lost their life preservers or planks while underwater, were grabbing frantically at the fragments of wreckage as they broke off and floated up to the surface.

Finally Mr. George saw the lights of the *Ellen*. He said later:

I never felt so thankful in all my life, for I never knew before what real gratitude was. I do not know whether or not I cried, but I know that I was astonished to hear my own laughter ringing in my ears. I do not know why I laughed. The verse, "God moves in a mysterious way," kept passing in and out of me—through me rather, as if I had been the pipe of an organ.

I never had the slightest doubt but that I would be saved until the lights passed by, and receded in the distance. Then I began to give myself up for lost indeed. But I slowly drifted toward her, until I could make out her hull and then a mast, and I shouted, and was taken up. When I got on the deck I could not stand. I did not know until then how exhausted I was.

The most remarkable individual experience was that of Fireman Alexander Grant. Though but a young man, this was his fourth shipwreck!

When a boy he had been wrecked on a Fall River schooner in the Bay of Fundy and barely saved his life. Later he was fireman aboard the ill-fated Collins steamer *Arctic* in 1854, and when she sank he floated away from her on a piece of lumber. He was picked up after several days of suffering by the ship *Cambria*. Then, as fireman on the *Crescent City*, he was rescued after that vessel crashed ashore in the Bahamas.

Now, for the fourth time, he was shipwrecked, and, just as the *Central America* went down, he and nine others clambered on part of the hurricane deck, a fragment of which they had previously cut clear.

That night they spent on the deck, praying and watching for another craft. They sighted one, the *Marine*, in the morning, but although they made every possible effort to attract the attention of those aboard, they were not seen.

All day and night they scanned the seas in vain. During Sunday morning eight people perished when they were washed off the raft. Then Monday morning young Grant rescued George W. Dawson from a log, and later picked up a second man. The raft later fell in with a passenger on a fragment of what once had been the captain's stateroom.

On the following day only Grant and Dawson were on the deck, the others having fallen off. That same afternoon, the third since the sinking, Grant sighted a boat in the distance.

I saw a boat three miles off, but could not tell whether there was anyone in it or not, but thought there was. Jumping into the sea I swam toward the boat with all my might. I discovered a man sitting in the boat, trying to scull the boat toward me.

On reaching the side of the boat, the man, who proved to be a Mr. Tice, helped me in. When secured by Mr. Tice, the lifeboat had been full of water. It had been bailed out by him through the aid of a bucket and tin pan which he had found in it, in addition to three good oars, which remained in the boat after being swamped.

Mr. Tice and I immediately pulled the boat as fast as possible to the hurricane deck, and took Mr. Dawson in. We allowed the boat to drift with the wind to seaward, not being able to help ourselves if we had wished, and not knowing which way to pull.

The three men saw a sail on Sunday, the eighth day after the shipwreck, but she disappeared over the horizon. On the ninth day they sighted the brig *Mary* which eventually rescued them.

The three survivors mentioned above who had been rescued by the brig *Mary* actually had drifted no less than 450 miles in the nine days since the *Central America* foundered.

For days afterward, ships searched the area for possible survivors still alive in the water, but none was found.

Now, more than a century later, fantastic stories of how the treasures of gold on the *Central America* were ignored may interest the average reader more than an accounting of how many were saved, although human life should always be considered as more valuable than gold. When the *Central America* sank to the bottom off the coast of North Carolina, she carried 444 victims, including brave Captain Herndon, to their death in the sea. Thus, of the total ship's company of 575, only 131 survived!

The passengers who ignored all the gold and gold dust aboard the *Central America* later told of the strange experience which they went through with thousands of dollars all around them. Never before in maritime history had there been such a large amount of money lying untouched in the main saloon of a ship. While the freight lists totaled well over $1,750,000, there were many who in their stateroom counted their wealth in gold by the tens of thousands.

As the storm raged and grew worse, the importance of the fortune seemed to diminish hourly until on Saturday even wealthy men tore off their treasure belts and scattered the gold around the deck of the saloon. In some instances full purses, containing thousands of dollars lay untouched. Carpet bags were opened, and the shining metal poured out onto the deck with abandon. One of the passengers opened up his bag and dashed $20,000 in gold on the deck, offering it to anyone who wished. It went untouched.

Thus, when the proud steamer sank to her doom, more than two and a third million in gold went with her. As gold is not affected by immersion in the ocean, it still lies at the bottom of the sea, awaiting some carefully planned diving expedition to bring the treasure up to the surface again.

PART II

WRECKS IN NEW ENGLAND
WATERS

⚓

CHAPTER FOUR

The *Watch and Wait*

⚓

The *Watch and Wait* was lost off the Massachusetts coast in the mighty storm of August 1635. Few readers know of the great hurricane which hit the New England coast more than three and a quarter centuries ago, on August 14, 1635. There are not many sources to which we can refer in covering this epic storm of the days of the Pilgrims and Puritans, but two men did record their experiences in that terrific gale. Anthony Thacher and William Bradford have left references to the tempest in their writings.

Thacher's Island itself is named because of the shipwreck of Anthony Thacher during that wild gale along the New England shores. It was onto this island off Gloucester, Massachusetts, that the tiny pinnace * *Watch and Wait* was hurled during the first great storm for which we have records.

* A pinnace is a small light vessel, usually two masted and schooner rigged.

Shortly after the wreck, Thacher wrote to his brother, Peter, telling the complete story of this early shipping disaster. The pinnace, which ran regularly up and down the coast, was owned by Isaac Allerton and stopped at many settlements between Piscataqua and Boston. This was the vessel on which Thacher planned to take passage. The Reverend John Avery and Anthony Thacher were cousins and had sworn "a league of perpetual friendship," which included an agreement never to forsake each other. Avery, formerly a preacher of Wiltshire, England, came to Newbury in 1634. The residents of Marblehead notified Avery that they were anxious for him to assume leadership of their church, so the minister made plans to move there with his family and Anthony Thacher's household.

The pinnace *Watch and Wait* on its trip down the coast stopped at Ipswich, August 11, 1635, to pick up eleven members of the Avery family, the seven members of the Thacher clan and a William Eliot, "sometimes of New Sarum." Four mariners manned the craft, and after proper religious observances, she was soon on the high seas bound for Marblehead. Nothing of importance occurred until the night of August 14, when a gale hit the vessel, ripping apart the sails. The crew refused to go aloft in the darkness of that night, as the wind and waves had created an angry sea, so the captain dropped anchor until morning.

Before the sun came up, the tempest had increased until it blew a veritable gale. Thacher says that even the Indians could not recall a fiercer blow than the storm which caught the pinnace off Cape Ann. Possibly it was the worst hurricane in all New England history. The anchors on the *Watch and Wait* began to drag and then snapped completely. The horrified crew and passengers were helpless to act. Anthony Thacher tells us in his own words what followed:

My cousin and I perceived our danger, solemnly recommended ourselves to God, the Lord both of earth and seas,
expecting with every wave to be swallowed up and drenched
in the deeps. And as my cousin, his wife, and my tender babes,
sat comforting and cheering one the other in the Lord against
ghastly death, which every moment stared us in the face, and
sat triumphing upon each one's forehead, we were by the
violence of the waves and fury of the winds (by the Lord's
permission) lifted up upon a rock between two high rocks,
yet all was one rock, but it raged with the stroke which came
into the pinnace, so as we were presently up to our middle in
water as we sat. The waves came furiously and violently over
us, and against us; but by reason of the rock's proportion
could not lift us off, but beat her all to pieces. Now look with
me upon our distress, and consider of my misery, who beheld
the ship broken, the water in her, and violently overwhelming us, my goods and provisions swimming in the seas, my
friends almost drowned, and mine own poor children so un-
timely (if I may so term it without offense) before my eyes
drowned, and ready to be swallowed up, and dashed to pieces
against the rocks by the merciless waves, and myself ready to
accompany them.

The captain resigned himself to the elements. The foremast went by the boards, the mainmast snapped into three
pieces, and the hull began to break up. When the waves
smashed into the cabin, the children started to cry frantically,
while the older people knelt in prayer. One of the sailors was
washed overboard and then into the cabin, striking against
Thacher. Aroused by the impact, Thacher looked out of the
cabin to see trees on a nearby island. The captain, determined
to find out what the land was, went out on deck, and was
drowned. The sailor who had washed against Thacher went
out, jumped into the water and started to swim to land. He,
too, was never seen again.

Commending themselves to the Lord, the two families

awaited the end of their sufferings. The children wept silently now, as all seemed resigned to their fate, whatever it might be. Suddenly a gigantic wave, much higher than any other, struck the weakened craft, sweeping Thacher, his daughter Mary, his cousin Avery and Avery's eldest son away. Anthony Thacher continues:

All the rest that were in the bark were drowned by the merciless seas. We four by that wave were swept clean away from off the rock also into the sea; the Lord, in one instant of time, disposing of fifteen souls of us according to his good pleasure and will. . . . God in his mercy caused me to fall by the stroke of one wave, flat on my face, for my face was toward the sea, insomuch that as I was sliding off the rock into the sea the Lord directed my toes into a joint in the rock's side, as also the tops of some of my fingers with my right hand, by means whereof, the waves leaving me, I remained so, having on the rock only my head above the water. . . . I stood bolt upright as if I had stood upon my feet, but I felt no bottom, nor had any footing for to stand upon but the waters.

Thacher grabbed at a fragment of the ship's mast, but missed it, and was washed along by the waves until he was beached on the island. His wife, caught in some of the wreckage, was also hurled up on the shore, and they discovered each other, alone of all the passengers and crew still alive. They thought of their five children, now gone from them, and Thacher blamed himself for taking them on the voyage. But Thacher tells us that they soon made plans for the future whatever it might bring:

I found a knapsack cast on the shore in which I had a steel, flint and powderhorn. Going further I found a drowned goat, then I found a hat, and my son William's coat, both of which I put on. My wife found one of her petticoats, which she put

on. I found also two cheeses, and some butter, driven ashore.
. . . So taking a piece of my wife's neckcloth which I dried in
the sun, I struck fire, and so dried and warmed our wet
bodies; and then skinned the goat, and having found a small
brass pot, we boiled some of her. Our drink was brackish
water; bread we had none.

There we remained until the Monday following; when,
about three of the clock in the afternoon, in a boat that came
that way, we went off that desolate island, which I named
after my name, Thacher's Woe, and the rock, Avery his Fall,
to the end that their fall and loss, and mine own, might be had
in perpetual remembrance. In the isle lieth the body of my
cousin's eldest daughter, whom I found dead on the shore.

The next day Thacher and his wife reached Marblehead.
Later their plans took them to Yarmouth, on Cape Cod,
where their three children, born after the disaster, continued
the family traditions. As a memorial to their ancestors, the
Thacher family have preserved a fragment of the cloth saved
from that wreck by their ancestor.

John Greenleaf Whittier describes the shipwreck off the
coast of Cape Ann in his *Swan Song of Parson Avery*.

There was a wailing in the shallop, woman's wail and man's
  despair,
A crash of breaking timbers on the rocks so sharp and bare,
And, through it all, the murmur of Father Avery's prayer.

There a comrade heard him praying, in the pause of wave
  and wind,
"All my own have gone before me, and I linger just behind;
Not for life I ask, but only, for the rest thy ransomed find!"

The ear of God was open to his servant's last request;
As the strong wave swept him downward, the sweet hymn
  upward pressed,
And the soul of Father Avery went singing to his rest.

Elsewhere along the coast there were other terrible disasters and occurrences. The tide rose to a height of twenty feet in the neighborhood of Buzzard's Bay and Providence. William Bradford, in his story of the Plimoth Plantation, tells of the great cyclone:

This year the 14, or 15, of August (being Saturday) was such a mighty storm of wind and raine as none living in these parts, either English or Indians, ever saw. Being like (for the time it continued) to those Hurricanes and Tuffoons that writers make mention in the Indies. It began in the morning, a little before day, and grue not be degrees, but came with a violence in the beginning, to the great amasmente of many. . . . It continued not (in the extremities) above 5. or 6. hours, but the violence began to abate. The signes and marks of it will remaine this 100. years in these parts where it was sorest.

CHAPTER FIVE

The Immigrant Ship *Saint John*

⚓

The most serious shipwreck to occur in the outer reaches of Boston Harbor was that of the British brig *Saint John* in the year 1849. One hundred and forty-three persons perished in this disaster, which took place inside of Minot's Ledge October 7 of that year. The *Saint John* had left Galway, Ireland, on September 5 for Boston, running into heavy weather off Cape Cod a month later.

The storm itself was well remembered around New England for many years. Rain began to fall October 6 late in the afternoon, and by midnight a violent storm from the northeast set in. Many other vessels were wrecked at various locations along the coast, while in Chelsea, Massachusetts, the walls of the partly constructed Universalist Church on Chestnut Street blew down with a terrific crash. Many other cities and towns in Massachusetts were swept by the gale, and the damage was exceedingly heavy.

When the weather turned thick, Captain Oliver of the *Saint John* ordered the crew to heave to, heading northeast. At four the next morning they wore ship and stood south. Several hours later Captain Oliver reached a point off Minot's Ledge Light and noticed the British brig *Kathleen* anchored just off Cohasset.

Hoping to gain the protection of a landlocked harbor, Oliver ran before the wind, dropping anchor near the newly completed but unlighted Minot's Ledge Lighthouse. The wind increased, the waves grew higher, and soon the *Saint John* began to drag her anchors. Although the frightened crew cut away the masts, the Irish immigrant ship slowly but inevitably neared the rocks. Suddenly a wave higher than the rest loomed before the terrified passengers and crew. Of gigantic proportions, the breaker rolled in toward the vessel, carrying the brig with its screaming cargo toward the rocky ledge.

Hundreds were watching the disaster from the Cohasset shore, while many others stood at the Glades House in Scituate. As they saw the vessel ready to pile up on the Grampus, they knew that the brig was doomed. They also realized that since the waves were too high to launch a lifeboat, few would be saved from the *Saint John*. The men of Cohasset and Scituate could do nothing except wait for the elements to subside.

Ripping and grinding its way over the outer rocks, the *Saint John* wallowed in the trough of the sea, buffeted by each wave as it swept by. Directly in its path was the Grampus, the grave of many a sturdy ship. With a tearing crash, the *Saint John* struck the ledge and began to break up.

The towering breakers swept over the vessel, twenty and thirty feet high, each wave carrying several victims to their death until only a few remained alive aboard the wreck. The ringbolt holding the jolly boat in place snapped, dropping the small craft into the ocean. Twenty-five persons jumped into the frail boat, which capsized, throwing the occupants into the sea. Only the captain and one boy managed to swim back to the ship, while all the others perished. A great wave now swept the longboat some distance from the ship, and a number of passengers drowned trying to swim to it. The captain and eleven others reached it, landing at the Glades an hour later after a dangerous trip through the high waves.

Meanwhile, the seas were going down rapidly, and a rescue boat from the shore started for the wreck. Rowing through the waves, they passed the captain and the others in the longboat, and decided from the fact that only twelve were in it that all others aboard the *Saint John* had been rescued. So the lifesavers rowed on by the wreck and headed for the British brig *Kathleen*. They had not seen the survivors aboard the *Saint John* because of the high waves.

Two incidents should be mentioned here. An Irishman, Patrick Swaney by name, was aboard the *Saint John* with his eleven children, and they were all swept overboard by the same wave. Swaney, with his youngest child at his breast, swam toward the longboat. When he had almost reached his destination, a gigantic wave engulfed him, and neither he nor the child was ever seen again. Since all the other children had pershed, that was the end of the Swaney family. A fourteen-year-old Irish lad had secreted himself aboard the emigrant ship at the start of the journey because his two sisters were going to America. When the crash came, he jumped into the jolly boat, swam back when it was swamped, and was later helped into the longboat. On reaching shore he discovered that both his sisters had been lost.

The great shipwreck off Cohasset attracted the attention of Henry David Thoreau, who was planning to visit Cape Cod. When the regular boat failed to run because of the storm,

Thoreau went by land, stopping at Cohasset. On the train he noticed many Irish people on their way to the scene. Arriving at Cohasset, he made his way through Cohasset common. As Thoreau walked by the graveyard, he saw an immense hole freshly dug there, where the bodies of the victims were to be placed.

Reaching the ocean, Thoreau found the sea still breaking violently over the rocks. More than twenty-six bodies had been recovered from the vessel. A woman who came to Boston without her baby months before had been expecting her sister to bring the child with her aboard the *Saint John*. On hearing of the tragedy she went down to the scene for particulars. The men in charge advised her to examine the remains of those who had come ashore. As the mother opened the lid of one of the coffins she found her own child in her sister's arms, both cold in death. The poor lady died three days later as a result of this terrible shock.

The men who worked straight through all the excitement made a deep impression on Thoreau as they continued collecting the seaweed as if nothing else mattered. Separating bits of cloth and sticks from it, the men piled up the kelp and rockweed undisturbed by the possibility of turning up a dead body at any time. Much debris filled the cove. A man's garments were arranged on a rock, then came a woman's scarf, a gown and a straw bonnet. A large section of the brig, forty feet long lying behind one of the rocks attracted Thoreau, and he climbed down to where he could examine the wreckage. Quoting from his story we read:

I was even more surprised at the power of the waves, exhibited on this shattered fragment, than I had been at the sight of the smaller fragments before. The largest timbers and iron braces were broken superfluously, and I saw that no material could withstand the power of the waves; that iron must go to pieces in such a case, and an iron vessel would be cracked up like an egg-shell on the rocks. Some of these timbers, however, were so rotten that I could almost thrust my umbrella through them. They told us some were saved on this piece, and also showed where the sea had heaved it into this cove which was now dry. When I saw where it had come in, and in what condition, I wondered that any had been saved on it. A little further on, a crowd of men was collected around the mate of the *St. John,* who was telling his story. He was a slim-looking youth, who spoke of the captain as the master, and seemed a little excited. He was saying that when they jumped into the boat she filled, and the vessel lurching, the weight of the water in the boat caused the painter to break, and so they were separated. Whereat one man came away saying,—"Well, I don't see but he tells a straight story enough. You see, the weight of the water in the boat broke the painter. A boat full of water is very heavy," —and so on, in a loud and impertinently earnest tone, as if he had a bet depending on it, but had no humane interest in the matter.

Another, a large man, stood near by upon a rock, gazing into the sea, and chewing large quids of tobacco, as if that habit were forever confirmed with him.

Further, we saw one standing upon a rock, who, we were told, was one that was saved. He was a sober-looking man, dressed in a jacket and gray pantaloons, with his hands in the pockets. I asked him a few questions, which he answered; but he seemed unwilling to talk about it, and soon walked away. By his side stood one of the lifeboat men, in an oil-cloth jacket, who told us how they went to the relief of the British brig, thinking that the boat of the *St. John,* which they passed on the way, held all her crew. . . . There were one or two houses visible from these rocks, in which were some of the survivors recovering from the shock which their bodies and minds had sustained. One was not expected to live.

We kept on down the shore as far as a promontory called

Whitehead, that we might see more of the Cohasset Rocks.
... We afterwards came to the lifeboat in its harbor, waiting
for another emergency; and in the afternoon we saw the
funeral procession at a distance, at the head of which walked
the captain with the other survivors.

Many years after the last bruised and battered body of the
immigrants had been placed in the Cohasset cemetery, the
Irish people of Boston visited the graveyard to dedicate a
graceful granite shaft in memory of the shipwrecked victims.
Because of this act of the Ancient Order of the Hibernians,
Patrick Swaney and his eleven children, as well as the others
who perished, will probably not be forgotten.

CHAPTER SIX

The *City of Columbus*

⚓

One of the most terrible marine disasters in the annals of Massachusetts steamship navigation was the loss of the Boston and Savannah liner *City of Columbus* at Martha's Vineyard in 1884, with the death of one hundred passengers and members of the crew.

When she sailed from Nickerson's Wharf * in Boston the steamer had eighty-seven passengers and a crew of forty-five. The *City of Columbus* possessed the highest rating possible, with an A-1 classification, and was amply provided with fixtures, life preservers and boats as required by law. It was a happy group of travelers who sailed away from Boston that January afternoon, for they were leaving the wintry weather for the South's warm, sunny climate.

As the steamer rounded Cape Cod, the night was clear and cold. The *City of Columbus*, all her lights visible, continued

* Nickerson's Wharf was across Northern Avenue Bridge in South Boston.

down the coast. The weather was getting colder, with a strong wind blowing from the northwest. By one thirty in the morning the captain, constantly on his feet since the ship had sailed, believed it safe to turn in. The dangerous part of the journey, around Cape Cod, lay behind, and the vessel was now halfway through Vineyard Sound. Captain S. C. Wright told his first mate, Edwin Fuller, the course to follow: "When Tarpaulan Cove bears north, change the course to west southwest."

It later developed that the man at the wheel, Quartermaster MacDonald, had not heard the low-voiced instructions the captain gave the first mate. Captain Wright then retired to his cabin in the rear of the pilothouse, but for some reason did not go to bed. He sat down on the floor with his back against a stanchion. The wind was now north northwest. Robert Bennet Forbes, master mariner of the nineteenth century, said later in referring to the ship that "any ordinary landsman without chart or compass could have taken her clear of all danger." The passage in the Vineyard Sound at this point is almost five miles wide, but the tired and overconfident mate did not realize that the combined force of wind and tide near Menemsha Bight was slowly dragging the great steamer to disaster.

At a few seconds before quarter of four that morning the lookout was pacing the deserted deck forward of the wheelhouse when he suddenly noticed a buoy on the starboard side of the ship. Shouting a warning at the top of his voice, he received no answer from the pilothouse, so rushed toward the man at the wheel. First Mate Fuller, however, hearing the cry, excitedly ordered Quartermaster MacDonald to port his helm.

The shouting aroused Captain Wright, who was still sitting on the floor of his cabin. Rushing into the wheelhouse, Wright cried out, "Hard a port!" and ordered the engines stopped. It was too late, for in less than thirty seconds the *City of Columbus* crashed on the hidden rocks of the Devil's Bridge at Martha's Vineyard, and disaster followed.

At this location there was a murderous double ledge which projected out underwater. The outer reef where the ship hit was locally known as the Devil's Back. And such it proved on that luckless night of 1884. The ship remained afloat barely four minutes after she hit, for the captain now made his greatest mistake.

"I . . . saw the buoy on the port side * about two points forward of beam and about three hundred yards distant," said the captain later. "She immediately struck. I ordered the engines reversed, and she backed out about twice her own length. The steamer stopped immediately, and I ordered the jib hoisted and endeavored to head her for the north, but she filled forward and listed to port so that the plant sluice was about four feet underwater."

Thus the captain ordered the vessel backed off the rocks which had ripped open the ship's bottom, and she sank at once. †

The *City of Columbus* crashed on the ledge at 3:45 that morning, and by ten minutes past four most of the men, women and children on the liner had perished. Number six lifeboat was launched but capsized at once. The crew lowered another boat which was crushed against the side of the ship. Four men later reached shore in it, however. Some of the men managed to set adrift one of the life rafts, but all aboard were swept off and drowned. Although a few survivors reached shore holding spars or woodwork, most of the others sank to their death in the icy waters.

The remaining twenty or so persons in the rigging suffered

* The hull was found inside the buoy.

† In 1887 the *Gate City* hit the same ledge, but stayed on, and no one was lost.

all the tortures that living people could endure. Frozen onto the shrouds because of the surf which lashed around them, and numbed by the zero wind which swept through their thin garments, the survivors, all men, waited for daylight. An hour after dawn the sufferers were gladdened when they saw smoke from a steamer which appeared around the west end of Cuttyhunk Island, dead to the windward of them. Four miles away, the ship was within easy view, and the watchers in the rigging counted the minutes before the vessel could arrive to save them. But their hopes were in vain. To their dismay, the steamer continued on her regular run up the coast, ignoring the now thoroughly discouraged victims. The ship had been the steamer *Glaucus,* commanded by Captain Bearse.

The keepers of the Gay Head Lighthouse had noticed a light out near the end of the Devil's Bridge and were organizing a crew to go to the wreck. Head Lighthouse Keeper Horace N. Pease had been called by his assistant at six that morning. Realizing that a shipwreck had taken place, Pease ordered Assistant Keeper Frederick Poole to make up a crew to row out to the scene. By dawn the attempt was begun. Poole had recruited lifesavers from the Gay Head Indians. Despite the heavy surf the lifeboat was launched into the breakers, but it soon overturned. All men reached the beach safely. Now soaking wet, their clothing was beginning to freeze. Poole ordered the men to remove their shoes and start out again in their stockings so their feet would not freeze. This time the lifeboat was successfully launched, and the dangerous waves were conquered. After an hour's struggle with the oars, the volunteers reached the scene of the wreck. Since the lifeboat would have capsized had it approached too close to the mast, the survivors, still clinging to the rigging, were told to jump into the water, where they would be picked up.

One by one the men in the shrouds jumped into the icy
waves, and each one was quickly rescued by the lifesavers.
The overcrowded lifeboat now started for land, but another
danger awaited the survivors. As the boat neared the shore,
a breaking wave swamped the craft, and she capsized just off
the beach. No one was drowned because of the quick work
of the Gay Head Indians, who pulled the shipwrecked victims out of the surf.

Meanwhile Keeper Pease had notified the residents of the
adjoining village of Squibnocket that a shipwreck had taken
place, and soon their volunteer lifesaving crew was on the
way to the wreck. They reached the scene and had rescued
several persons when a whistle in the distance drew their
attention to the revenue cutter *Dexter* steaming toward them
under forced draft. The Squibnocket lifeboat started for
shore with its load of humanity, leaving nineteen forms clinging to the rigging.

When two boats were sent over to the wreck from the
revenue cutter, seventeen more survivors dropped into the
sea and were saved. Only two persons could now be seen
clinging to the rigging. As it appeared that they were afraid
to leave the wreck, young Lieutenant Rhodes of the *Dexter*
volunteered to swim over to the *Columbus* to rescue the men.
With a rope around his waist, Rhodes jumped into the January seas. Swimming through the water, he was hit by some
floating wreckage and had to be hauled back to the *Dexter*.
Shortly afterward the wind went down, and Lieutenant
Rhodes made a second attempt, this time using the dinghy.
After trying unsuccessfully several times, Rhodes made the
dinghy fast to the rigging and began to climb the futtock
shrouds. When he reached the two men, he found that both
had frozen to death in the ratlines. Cutting the bodies down,
Rhodes dropped them into the water, later rowing back to
the revenue cutter with them. He left the wreck alone in the

sea, with its icy rigging glistening in the sun and its bow barely showing above the waves. One hundred lives had been sacrificed to carelessness. Estimates run from 99 to 109 on the number drowned.

Several of the men who were active either on the wreck or ashore have left their personal testimony of the disaster. One of these individuals was Quartermaster Roderick A. Mac-Donald, the man at the helm when the vessel struck. His testimony follows:

I went on duty at midnight. Heavy winds, clear, could see lights plainly, a little hazy on land. Wind a little on starboard bow. The usual course on passing Tarpaulin Light on Naushon is southwest by west, which should take us clear of the Sow and Pigs Lightship. We generally intend to steer in mid channel. The captain went below about three-quarters of an hour before the vessel struck, and gave me the course a quarter or half an hour before he went below. It was southwest by west. The second mate was in the pilot house when the course was given. The second mate told me a short time before she struck not to go to leeward of that course. . . . The light shone out plain enough but you could not judge the distance from the light. It appeared closer than usual but I was not in command of the ship. That is the course I always steer through there.

Quartermaster MacDonald, after the crash, was successful in swimming to the lifeboat which had floated some distance from the wreck, and took charge of operations to reach the island. Time after time the crew tried to row directly for the shore, where they would have drowned in the great breakers, but MacDonald prevailed upon them to keep off until the calmer waters of Menemsha Bight were reached. By this time one of the passengers in the lifeboat had died of exposure, but the craft was landed safely near the home of an Indian named Ryan, where the survivors were given the best of care.

The aftermath of the shipwreck of the *City of Columbus* included many touching scenes. Among the bodies found was that of a young woman with a tiny pair of shoes frozen to her breast, her child having been separated from her in the terrifying moments after the crash.

Captain Bearse of the *Glaucus* was later called before the investigation committee and asked why he had not bothered to sail over closer to the wreck of the *City of Columbus*. He admitted that he recognized the ship on the Devil's Bridge as the *City of Columbus,* but since he knew she had been supposed to pass that particular point hours before, he figured all the survivors had been removed from the ship. He said at the investigation that he looked through his telescope at the wreck and could see no movement of any kind. Although the United States marine inspectors exonerated Captain Bearse, Robert Bennet Forbes condemned their action as "lame and impotent." Captain Forbes said that it was because of a deplorable dullness of mind and vision that Bearse did not sail close enough to see the men in the rigging, where he could have saved the lives of many who subsequently perished.

Captain S. C. Wright, the master of the *Columbus,* was deprived of his license as pilot and his certificate as shipmaster. Many years later a prominent Boston sea captain was ashore at Savannah, Georgia. As he walked up the pier, stepping between bales of cotton and other cargo piled up ready for shipment, he heard a voice hailing him. Stepping closer, the Boston mariner recognized the former master of the *City of Columbus* working as a stevedore on the wharves at Savannah.

⚓︎

CHAPTER SEVEN

The Steamer *Portland*

⚓︎

Almost two-thirds of a century has elapsed since the beautiful white-and-gold-trimmed steamer *Portland* sailed from Boston on November 26, 1898, on her regular run to Portland, Maine. The paddle-wheel steamer, built at Bath, Maine, in 1890, was 291 feet long and of 42-foot beam. Since this trip took place the Saturday after Thanksgiving, there were more passengers than usual who wished to make the return journey to Portland that night. Many were returning to Maine from Philadelphia, New York and points south after spending the holiday with their families.

That November morning the weather was pleasantly fair, with a light breeze. As the day wore on, however, the clouds above Boston grew heavier, the first signs of a growing condition of grave danger. A tremendous cyclone from the Gulf of Mexico was about to join forces with a storm of only slightly lesser proportions roaring across from the Great Lakes.

Meanwhile, the loading of the steamer's freight continued at India Wharf in Boston. Passengers who had made reservations for the trip began to come aboard. Some of them later canceled their accommodations, but the majority, more than one hundred persons, sailed with the ship. With passengers and crew, there were 191 * people aboard the *Portland* by sailing time.

The general manager of the Portland Steam Packet Company, John F. Liscomb, received warning of the approaching storm from New York and tried to communicate by phone from Portland with the steamer's captain, Hollis H. Blanchard. Failing in this, he left word that the *Portland*'s companion ship, the newer *Bay State,* should not leave Portland until nine o'clock, when the size of the storm could be better gauged. When he returned at five-thirty, Blanchard talked over the phone to the *Bay State*'s captain, Alexander Dennison, called because of his comparative youthfulness "the Kid Pilot."

Captain Dennison repeated to Blanchard the manager's suggestion to hold the *Portland* until nine o'clock that night. Captain Blanchard replied that the *Portland* would sail on schedule at seven. He added that, judging by the direction of the storm, it would not reach the city of Portland until after the steamer had safely docked. Dennison, said Blanchard, would be proceeding southward and would run into the storm before he reached Boston. But Captain Blanchard, who had been ordered to sail that night, thought it wise for the *Portland* to sail on time so as to reach her destination before the storm.

The fact that the two captains talked over the phone that

* The numbers certified on Jan. 31, 1963.

day has given rise to the popular legend that Captain Blanchard sailed contrary to the advice of the general manager. The
motive ascribed to him was that he was anxious to prove his
professional superiority to Captain Dennison by steaming
into Portland Harbor while the *Bay State* was still at the
wharf. There seems to be no foundation in fact for this
rumor, though it dies hard.

There has always been a heated controversy as to whether
or not Captain Hollis H. Blanchard was ordered to sail that
night. A few years ago I interviewed Miss Grace Blanchard,
granddaughter of the captain. She told me that her father,
Charles Blanchard, visited his father shortly before the *Portland* left the pier and had a conversation with him. The two
men talked with each other briefly in the pilothouse.

"My father asked my grandfather if it was necessary for
him to sail," Miss Blanchard said. "The wind had started to
come up, and they knew there was a heavy snowstorm in New
York. Grandfather Blanchard said to his son, 'I have my
orders to sail, and I am going!' Those were the last words
ever spoken by my grandfather to a member of his family."

Captains of passenger vessels invariably feel the responsibility for the many lives which depend upon their skill and
judgment. Those who really knew Captain Blanchard were
convinced that he was no exception. His decision was based
upon long experience, and at least twelve other sea captains
have admitted that under similar conditions they would have
reasoned and acted as he did.

At 6:07, fifty-three minutes before sailing time, the final
notice arrived with the information that it was still snowing
in New York, but that the wind had backed around to northwest. This news gave Captain Blanchard further confidence
that he could reach Portland ahead of the storm as he had
done many times before. At precisely seven o'clock that November evening the final departing whistle from the *Portland*

split the chill night air of Boston's Atlantic Avenue, and Captain Hollis Blanchard sailed into the unknown.

It is falsely believed that the *Portland* was not seen after leaving Boston on her way up the coast. However, Captain William Thomas, of Bailey Island, Maine, master of the fisherman *Maud S.*, saw the lights of the *Portland* when he was nearly four miles southwest of Thacher's Island. Since his wife was supposedly on the steamer, Thomas was naturally watching for the ship with more than ordinary interest. From his vantage point less than two miles away from the side-wheeler, it seemed to Thomas that the steamer was closer to shore than usual. He said to his crew, "There goes the *Portland*. She will probably run close to Thacher's."

It was then two and a half hours after Blanchard had sailed from Boston. Nothing at that time led Thomas to believe that the captain of the *Portland* was foolhardy in continuing her journey.*

Captain A. A. Tarr, of Thacher's Island Light off Gloucester, agreed with Thomas about conditions at the time the *Portland* passed by. He said that the weather seemed so nearly normal when the ship was scheduled to pass the island that he did not even bother to look for the sparkle of her lights. We have the additional evidence of another man stationed at Thacher's Island. Captain Lynes B. Hathaway, of Brockton, master workman of the Lighthouse Department, at nine thirty or shortly thereafter saw the *Portland*'s lights as the steamer passed within five hundred feet of the shore between Thacher's and the Londoner Ledge. The *Portland*, then on schedule, continued up the coast.

Around eleven o'clock, less than ninety minutes after Captain Hathaway saw the steamer, Captain Reuben Cameron, of the schooner *Grayling*, sighted the *Portland* twelve miles

---

* Incidentally, Thomas's wife was not on the *Portland*, having made a fortunate use of the privilege of changing her mind.

south by east of Thacher's Island. Thus, without question, the vessel had changed her course. The *Portland* came so near to the *Grayling* that Captain Cameron burned a Coston flare to warn the steamer away. The paddle-wheeler at this time seemed to be rolling and pitching badly, although her superstructure appeared intact.

Also in the vicinity was the schooner *Florence E. Stream.* At approximately 11:15 P.M. she and her master, Captain Frank Stream, passed a paddle-wheel steamer which must have been the *Portland,* as there was no other vessel of her type in the area. Half an hour later Captain D. J. Pellier, of the schooner *Edgar Randall,* then fourteen miles southeast by east of Eastern Point, Gloucester, noticed a large vessel bearing down upon him out of the night. Pellier swung the *Randall* away and escaped a collision but had no time to see whether the ship was a paddle-wheel steamer. At the time, he believed that the steamer's superstructure had been damaged, but the accuracy of his vision from the lurching deck of a small schooner is a matter of conjecture.

Meanwhile the storm had increased in intensity. In Portland at noon there had been a north wind blowing at nineteen miles per hour, which increased at 2:00 P.M. to twenty-six, changing to northeast at three o'clock, then increasing to thirty-six miles an hour that evening. After swinging around to north at 6:00 P.M., the wind shifted to northeast an hour later. There were spells of wind which blew during this period at almost a mile a minute. In Boston the official records indicate that many gusts as high as seventy-two miles an hour were registered. Occasionally the velocity reached almost unbelievable intensity. The barometer at Boston dropped from 29.70 at seven to 29.44 at midnight.

Ships all along the coast scurried for shelter. Vessel after vessel, failing to reach a safe harbor, was tossed ashore along the southern and northern coast of Massachusetts, and every seaside town and city in the path of the storm was fearfully battered. Giant breakers swept through many main thorough-fares, and the tide, as measured at Cohasset, rose even higher than it had during the record gale of 1851 which toppled Minot's lighthouse.

Just how far on her scheduled journey did the *Portland* go? There were those, including the late yachting enthusiast and newsman, William U. Swan, who believed that the *Portland* reached a point north of Boon Island off Portsmouth on her voyage up the coast. This belief is hard to reconcile with the known facts. If the side-wheeler passed the Londoner Ledge off Thacher's Island around nine thirty, she could not have attained a position near Boon Island, many miles to the north, changed her course and still be twelve miles south-east of Thacher's Island ninety minutes later at 11:00 P.M. Logically it would seem that the *Portland* never sailed far-ther than five miles north of Thacher's Island on her sched-uled route.

Captain Frank Scripture, of Rockport, Massachusetts, later said that when the *Portland* sailed from Boston there was no reason why a prudent master should not leave that port. But Captain Scripture had never experienced a storm as sudden as the one which descended on Cape Ann that night. Prob-ably, when the blast caught Captain Blanchard somewhere north of Thacher's Island, he headed the *Portland* toward the open sea to ride out the gale as he had done before. Judging by what we know of the fate of the *Monticello* in another storm off Nova Scotia, it is possible and even prob-able that the *Portland* soon began shipping seas and then developed a list to starboard. The net result of the various conflicting forces in the gale placed the *Portland* off Cape Cod early the next day.

At five forty-five that Sunday morning, Keeper Samuel O. Fisher, of the Race Point Life Saving Station, heard four blasts from a steamer's whistle. He went out, glanced at the clock and rang the gong for the surfboat in case rescue work was ahead. Although he telephoned Peaked Hill Station to be on the lookout and sent a man down to the beach, neither ship nor wreckage could be seen at that time. "Conditions were the worst I have ever known," Keeper Fisher said later.

While neither Fisher nor his men saw any sign of the *Portland* early that morning, when the eye of the hurricane passed across Cape Cod between nine and ten thirty, several other persons saw the *Portland* wallowing in the huge offshore seas some five to eight miles from Cape Cod during a brief clearing in the skies. The clear weather lasted until ten thirty, and then the storm returned with all its former fury. By two o'clock it was worse than ever.

At the end of the afternoon, the bitter wind continued to fill the air with snow and sand, making it nearly unbearable for Surfman John Johnson, of the Peaked Hill Bars Station, as he plodded along the beach. He knew that another lifesaver was pushing toward him from the Race Point Coast Guard Station several miles away and that ahead was the Half Way House which marked the division of their patrol. Arriving at the Half Way House, Johnson met his fellow watchman, Surfman Bickers, exchanged a story or two, spoke of the gale and started back along the windswept beach.

The darkness increased. At seven-twenty Johnson thought he saw something thrown up by the incoming tide. Keeping his eye on the object, he fought his way down to the shore, picked up his find and hastily retreated to the bank above the surf. In the dim light of his lantern he examined the object. It was a life belt, and on it he read the words *Steamer Portland of Portland.* He had no reason to suppose anything more than that the boat had lost a life preserver.

Here is his statement:

I was bound west toward the station, when I found the first thing that landed from the steamer. It was a life belt and it was one-half mile east of the station. At seven-forty-five o'clock that evening I found the next seen wreckage, a creamery can, forty-quart, I guess. It was right below our station, and nine or ten more of them, all empty and stoppered tightly came on there closely together.

Jim Kelly succeeded me on the eastern beat, leaving the station at eight-twenty P.M. and at nine-thirty he found doors and other light woodwork from the *Portland* on the shore. When I found the life belt the wind was north northeast.

Actually, the *Portland* was at that time in the last stages of foundering. Thomas Harrison Eames tells us that "the pounding of the sea under her guards opened her up and allowed tons of water to rush into the hull, flooding engine room and boiler room, drowning the men and depriving the ship of her power."

It was not until eleven o'clock, around high tide, that the wreckage began to come ashore in large quantities. Edwin B. Tyler, of the Race Point crew, found doors, electric light bulbs, wash stand tops and other wreckage, and when the midnight watch returned, the beach was buried with debris from the *Portland*. Mattresses, chairs, upholstery, windows, doors and paneling all came ashore just before midnight.

The next morning the Cape Cod shore was littered with wreckage piled eight and ten feet high. In with the *Portland*'s remains were fragments from the ninety-six-foot granite schooner *Addie E. Snow,* which had also gone down with all hands. A short distance away the upper part of the cabin from the steamer *Pentagoet* was discovered embedded in the sand. The wreck of the *Snow* was later discovered a short distance from the *Portland* on the bottom of the sea. Thirty-six bodies were eventually recovered and identified from the

Portland, but not one body was ever found from either the *Snow* or the *Pentagoet.*

Several watches found on the victims had stopped at about nine-fifteen, and since the *Portland* was definitely seen afloat later than that on Sunday morning, we can safely assume that she made her final plunge around quarter past nine that Sunday night, November 27, 1898.

Because the wreckage of the *Addie E. Snow* and the *Portland* came up on the beach together, it is entirely possible that a collision may have occurred between the two vessels. An engine room gong with a lignum vitae clapper, attached to a bulkhead, later floated to the surface and was brought into Boston. In order for this to be freed from the engine room in the bowels of the ship, the *Portland* must have split apart before she sank, as the *Monticello* did when she went down off Nova Scotia. The question is: Did the *Portland* break in two because of a collision or did she split in two of her own accord? Probably this will never be answered.

Relics from the *Portland* are many. I have heard that there is scarcely a cottage along the Outer Beach at Cape Cod that does not have its *Portland* souvenir. There are said to be four wheels of the *Portland* in existence. The captain's speaking trumpet was sold to a westerner in 1899, and an oil dealer converted a life raft into a container from which to sell kerosene on the streets of Boston. Cy Young, of Hyannis, amassed a great amount of *Portland* material, storing empty coffins, cabin posts, bunks, doors and life belts in the cellar of his antique shop in Provincetown, where he sold them for forty-five years after the disaster. Hundreds of paper knives and miniature oars were carved from stateroom blinds and doors, and stateroom door numbers commanded a high premium. Today, although sixty-five years have elapsed since the disaster, these relics are seldom sold but are handed down as precious heirlooms from generation to generation.

Through the years, relatives and friends of those lost aboard the side-wheeler have been drawn together by a common bond. It was their custom to meet in Boston at India Wharf, from which the *Portland* sailed, and hold memorial services for their loved ones. The group became known as the *Portland* Associates. On each anniversary at precisely seven o'clock in the evening, one of the members read the the names of those who were lost. With the reading of the final name, another member dropped flowers into the harbor from the pier. Then those assembled would discuss their individual versions of the weather that fateful night or repeat to each other their own anxieties and emotions when they first realized the *Portland* was missing.

At the first report that the steamer had not been heard from, mild alarm had given way to doubt, then deep anxiety and, finally, the cold, gripping fear which accompanied the awesome certainty that their loved ones and the *Portland* had been lost at sea. The *Portland* story became one which has been told and retold with undying interest through the years.

The late John A. Thornquist, of Medford, was the president of the group when the fiftieth anniversary was held in 1948. Eighty persons gathered that evening on India Wharf. Then, at 7:00 P.M., exactly fifty years after the *Portland* had sailed from that same wharf, the exercises began. The names were read, prayers were given and flowers were scattered into the sea. The next day President Thornquist led a smaller group to Highland Light, Cape Cod, where in the presence of many Cape Codders he unveiled a tablet to the *Portland* victims. The memorial plaque was placed against the sturdy sides of Highland Light, overlooking the waters where the side-wheeler plunged to her doom fifty years before.

Miss Marie Hansen, of Cambridge, has been the president of the Sons and Daughters of the Portland Associates since

1956. Miss Hansen recently told me that there are now 191 names of persons on the list of victims of the disaster, a list now at the Old State House in Boston. Although the list stood at 190 for many years, the name of George Luther Prescott has recently been added.

Hundreds of persons who were in Boston when the *Portland* sailed claimed that they planned to be aboard her but for one reason or another were delayed and missed the boat. Some say that they were in a barroom taking a last drink, others that they were on a streetcar which was held up. My only comment is that the barrooms and streetcars of Boston must have been packed with humanity that day, judging by the great numbers who have chosen to identify themselves with the *Portland* in this manner. Actually, of course, there were only a few authentic cases of persons who did not sail as they had planned. The story of Mrs. Anna Young of Boston is one of the true accounts:

I was resting in my stateroom. The whistle of the *Portland* was sounding for all visitors to go ashore. Suddenly there was a knock at the door, and a message from my mother was delivered. Mother believed a storm was coming, and she had a premonition that I shouldn't sail. Carrying my child, I ran for the gangplank just as they started to lift it, and they waited for me. When I got ashore I heard the final whistle of the Portland as she left the wharf.

Another true story of a lucky hunch was told by Mr. George Gott, of Brooklin, Maine. Mr. Gott was standing on the wharf before going aboard the steamer when he noticed the strange behavior of the ship's cat. She was systematically removing her litter of kittens from the ship to a corner of a great barnlike shed on the wharf. Again and again she boarded the vessel and brought another kitten ashore. Then and there Mr. Gott decided that if the *Portland* wasn't good enough for the ship's cat that night, it wasn't good enough for him, and the side-wheeler sailed without him.

For the past thirty years I have been collecting information about the steamer *Portland*. I have in my possession letters from several of those whose information was vital in piecing together what we knew about the side-wheeler. Many other letters, more than four hundred, in fact, mentioned the possibility of getting a diver to go down to the *Portland* and examine her.

In 1944, I visited Captain Charles G. Carver in Rockland, Maine, who told me of his contact with the *Portland*. He had been scallop-dragging about five miles north of Highland Light around the year 1932 and brought to the surface a lot of material which was identified as coming from the *Portland*. A short distance away he also located a small granite schooner, probably the *Addie E. Snow*. His interest centered on the *Portland,* however.

"I have no doubt but that we had our drags on what is now left of the steamer *Portland*," Captain Carver told me. He mentioned pulling up six champagne bottles, several door knobs, dishes, plates, silverware and frame fixtures. One doorknob had the insignia of the old Portland Steam Packet Company engraved on the handle. Since the *Portland* was the only vessel of that line lost off Cape Cod, I felt sure that he must have been over the wreck of the ill-fated side-wheeler.

Captain Carver examined his records to give me the exact location of the *Portland,* and I made plans to send a diver down to the hull of the vessel. (Not one of those who had suggested that I arrange for diving operations volunteered to help financially in the project.) I contracted with diver Al George, of Malden, Massachusetts, to descend to the hull of the old steamer. He spent the last week of June and the first day of July 1945 working at the location, after which he prepared and signed a statement covering the vital part of his diving activities. His account follows:

In the month of June, 1945, I was commissioned by Lt. Edward R. Snow to descend to the bottom of the ocean off Cape Cod at a location previously found by Captain Charles G. Carver of Rockland, Maine. Highland Light is at a distance of 4½ miles; the Pilgrim Monument, has a bearing of 210 degrees; Race Point Coast Guard Station is seven miles distant.

Arriving on the location during the last week of June, I carried out the plans for finding the *Portland*. I ran a course 115 degrees true from the Peaked Hill Bar Buoy. I made a sweep after reaching a point 1¾ miles from the buoy, using a span of 600 feet of cable. We swept the entire location within a radius of three-quarters of a mile. On the second time across I made fast to what I knew was some large submerged object. After buoying it, we swept the entire vicinity to make sure the object was the steamer *Portland* and not some other wreck. Of this I am certain: This wreck is the only wreck in this vicinity which corresponds to the bearings given by Captain Carver. Therefore it must be the steamer *Portland*.

Realizing this fact, I then got rigged for diving. I slid down the sweep wire and within three minutes of the time I had left the *Regavlas* I had landed on the *Portland* which was over on its beam ends and heavily sanded in. It may surprise the average person to realize that the visibility here is less than 18 inches.

It was a weird sight. Crawling along the sloping hull of the vessel, I nosed my helmet forward until I ran into a mast heavily covered with marine growth (mussels, seaweed, etc.). Reaching my hands out, I found I could not span the mast. I followed the mast up until it went off out of my reach at a space between two gigantic boulders on the bottom. The mast appeared to be broken off 15 feet up.

It would seem as though the *Portland* had hit bottom on

her beam ends and then through the years had worked its way into the sand until it is buried almost completely. Only the bare hull of the ship seems in position.

All superstructure evidently has been spread around the ocean bed long ago. The boulders are much higher than my head. I could not tell whether it was the foremast or the mainmast. Going down on my hands and knees, I could make out the ripples of sand on the bottom of the sea and could see little shells from time to time.

The tide was running about one knot and it was slack water. My brother telephoned down from upstairs that he had 300 feet of line run out to enable me to stand on bottom in 144 feet of water.

It was a strange experience standing there alone with the ill-fated *Portland* and probably what remained of the passengers and crew still imprisoned in her sand-covered hull.

I wish I could give one the awesome picture. While visibility was a foot and a half, vague shadows could be made out up to five and eight feet away. Giant devil weed and long streamers of other varieties of seaweed shrouded me in a big black cloud of marine life.

As there probably will be many who might think that the *Portland* sank gently to the bottom to remain practically intact for the forty-seven years since the disaster, I must impress on their minds the true picture of the present conditions. The entire hull of the vessel which protrudes above the sand is a blackened shapeless mass of watersoaked wood, seaweed, mussels, scallops and scores of different types of marine growth.

I spent less than a half hour on the bottom, then I gave the signal to be hoisted up to twenty feet from the surface where I hung for ten minutes, then I was hoisted to ten feet from the surface where I remained for fifteen minutes. I was then brought over the side and my dive had been completed.

I realize that the purser's bell, the keys, the doorknobs and the many other articles which have been brought to the surface from this shipwreck indicate many more articles could be retrieved. I have been told that a small fortune in uncut gems in the purser's safe would well repay the lucky finder. In my opinion, however, although I would be happy to undertake the search, the chances are greatly against anything more of practical value ever being found. If anyone would consider financing such an enterprise, the cost would be prohibitive.

AL GEORGE

Each year I receive more letters from *Portland* enthusiasts. Many of the writers suggest that I conduct further research work on the hull of the steamer, at my own expense, and thereby find the purser's safe. It has been said that the safe contains many uncut diamonds, but I am extremely skeptical, and even if the diamonds were there, the chances that they would be found are small.

Perhaps it is just as well to let the old steamer rest for the remainder of her existence at the bottom of the sea, undisturbed by visits from the world above the surface. There is much that we should like to know for certain about the sidewheeler, but the chances are greatly against the appearance of new information at this date. In any event, the last voyage of the *Portland* will remain forever one of New England's greatest sagas of the sea.

CHAPTER EIGHT

The Monomoy Disaster

An event which excited much popular sympathy over the entire country in the year 1902 was the disaster which befell the Monomoy lifesaving boat as she neared the beach at Monomoy Point, south of Chatham, Massachusetts, on the morning of March 17. Together with the subsequent rescue of the sole survivor, Surfman Ellis, by Captain Elmer Mayo, the event created an unusual amount of interest, especially around New England.

Two coal barges, the *Wadena* and the *Fitzpatrick,* had been stranded in a storm several days before on the Shovelful Shoal off Monomoy Point, and several men were rescued by the Monomoy Lifesaving Crew. The weather moderated, allowing wreckers to go aboard and plan the task of lightering the vessels. On the evening of March 16 the weather grew heavy, so that all but a few men were taken ashore by the tug *Peter Smith.*

The next morning when the barge *Wadena* flew a distress signal, Captain Eldridge organized a lifeboat crew to reach the craft. At several places on the shoals the seas were extremely rough, but the surfboat reached the lee of the barge without incident. With a line made fast, plans were formed for the return journey. Five men were on the barge, all of whom excitedly asked to be taken ashore. It is believed that the workers on the *Wadena* were in a partial state of panic from their perilous position.

Four of the five men lowered themselves into the boat successfully, but the captain of the barge, a heavy man, let go his hold when he was a few feet above the lifeboat, and crashed into the after thwart, breaking it. The painter was cut as soon as the five men had been placed in postion in the lifeboat, and the trip to safety began. The surfmen began to row in a steady cadence, but emerging from the lee of the *Wadena,* the lifeboat was hit by a great wave which partly filled the craft. This made the bargemen frantic, and they leaped to their feet, throwing their arms about the surfmen, crying for help. One after another the waves struck the little lifeboat until it finally filled and capsized with its thirteen occupants. Twice the craft was righted by the surfmen in the water, but each time the seas overturned her.

The five bargemen were the first to drown, since they made no effort to get back to the overturned lifeboat. The surfmen clung desperately to the bottom of the boat, but soon their strength began to fail. Surfman Chase was the first to perish, and then Nickerson and Small disappeared. Only five now remained. Ellis, who was the sole survivor, later wrote down his experience:

Captain Eldridge, Surfmen Kendrick, Foye and Rogers and myself still managed to hold to the boat. Every sea which struck the boat swept completely over us, almost smothering us. Kendrick was the next one of our crew to perish, and poor Foye soon followed him. Captain Eldridge and Surfman Rogers and myself were the only ones left and we expected that we, too, would soon share the fate of our comrades.

Rogers was clinging to the boat about amidships, while Captain Eldridge and myself were holding on near the stern. Captain Eldridge called to me to help him get a better hold, and I managed to pull him on to the bottom of the boat, when a sea struck us and washed us both off. I managed to regain a hold on the bottom of the boat, and looking around for Captain Eldridge, I saw that he was holding on to the spar and sail which had drifted from underneath the boat, but was still fast to it. The seas were washing me off the boat continually at this time, and when I last saw our brave captain, he was drifting away from the boat holding on to the spar and the sail.

My strength was fast going, and when poor Rogers begged me to help him climb further up onto the boat, the only thing I could do was to tell him that we were drifting toward the beach, and that help would soon be at hand and to hang on.

Rogers had lost his strength, however, and failing to get a more secure place on the bottom of the boat, feebly moaning, "I have got to go," he fell off the boat and sank beneath the waters.

I was now alone on the bottom of the boat, and seeing that the center board had slipped part way out, I managed to get hold of it, and holding it with one hand had succeeded in getting my oil clothes, undercoat, vest and boots off.

By that time the overturned boat had drifted down over the shoals in the direction of the barge *Fitzpatrick,* which was also stranded on the shoals, and when I sighted the craft I waved my hand as a signal for help. I soon saw those on the barge fling a dory over the side into the water, but could see nothing more of the dory after that until it hove in sight with a man in it rowing towards me.

The man in the dory was Captain Elmer F. Mayo. At the time of the Monomoy disaster, he was aboard the barge *Fitzpatrick* in company with Captain Mallows, of Chatham, and the barge captain. There had been a fourteen-foot dory alongside the barge, which was hauled on deck the night before. The only oars aboard were too long for the dory, so Mayo cut them down.

Mayo knew nothing of the tragedy until he noticed Surfman Ellis drifting along, clinging to the overturned lifeboat. Realizing that a catastrophe had occurred, Mayo stripped down to his underwear, let over the dory and climbed down a rope into the little craft.

With improvised tholepins and oars so large he could hardly hold them, Mayo fought his way toward the lifeboat. Surfman Ellis saw the dory just as it reached him. It was a difficult feat to take Ellis from the water, but as both men were experts at the task of lifesaving, it was successfully accomplished. Mayo realized that Ellis could not stand the exposure much longer and headed the dory for shore at once. Only his expert knowledge of the shoals and rips around Monomoy allowed Mayo to reach the shore where Surfman Walter Bloomer rushed into the breakers to assist in beaching the dory. The two men were quickly cared for.

Mayo's feat had been one of outstanding heroism earning for him the title "Hero of Monomoy." Both the United States and the Massachusetts Humane Society recognized Mayo's gallantry, awarding him medals for his rescue.

The people of New England quickly responded to a call for help for the widows of the Monomoy lifesavers. William U. Swan, then of the Associated Press, publicized the story throughout the nation, and a benefit meeting was held at the

Tremont Theatre, Boston, where Ellis, Mayo and the Mayo's dory were on view. In a comparatively short time a fund of $36,583.52 was raised for the widows of the men who sacrificed their lives that wintry morning off Cape Cod.

CHAPTER NINE

The *Larchmont* Disaster

Often we find that history teaches but man disregards the lesson. It is the same way with marine disasters. When the *Portland* sank off Cape Cod in 1898 carrying the only passenger list, tremendous agitation developed for requiring an extra list to be left ashore whenever a passenger vessel sailed from port. Yet in 1907, more than eight years after the *Portland* storm, the Joy liner *Larchmont* left her pier in Providence, Rhode Island, with the only passenger list available. Evidently the steamship lines of that period had learned nothing from bitter experience, continuing a policy which had caused the general public such indignation. The era of which we write has gone; today maritime regulations are better than in any other period in the nation's history.

It was at seven o'clock in the evening on February 11, 1907, that the *Larchmont* left Providence, almost half an hour behind her regular schedule. The wind was about northwest,

blowing nearly forty miles an hour, when Captain G. W. Mc-
Vey took the steamer down the river. As the *Larchmont* approached Sabine Point, McVey gave charge of the wheel to
Quartermaster Staples, under the supervision of Mr. Anson,
the First Pilot.

Captain McVey now proceeded on his usual tour of the
ship, after which he called on the ship's purser. At about
quarter of eleven he passed through the pilothouse, where he
conversed briefly with the man at the wheel. The pilot was in
command of the course to be steered. The steamer's headlight,
masthead light and side lights were all burning brightly, and
everything was in satisfactory order.

Shortly before eleven fifty when Watch Hill Light bore
four miles northwest, Quartermaster Staples, at the wheel,
saw the lights of a schooner ahead. The vessel was yawing and
luffing, making it hard to figure her course. As she appeared
on the starboard side of the *Larchmont,* Staples swung his
wheel hard-a-port, but evidently the schooner, later identified
as the *Harry Knowlton,* luffed just at that time, for the
schooner's red light disappeared completely. The *Knowlton*
was even then headed directly for the doomed *Larchmont,*
crashing a moment later into the steamer's starboard side just
forward of amidships.

As the schooner bore down on the steamer, several short,
rapid blasts of the steam whistle were sounded from the
wheelhouse of the *Larchmont,* bringing Captain McVey from
his cabin into the pilothouse just as the schooner loomed up
and smashed against his vessel. Captain McVey's own story
follows:

Realizing that this was a severe blow, I at once rang the bell
to call the engineer so as to have him report to me the conditions of affairs below. Failing to get any response, I at once
sent Mr. Wyman, who had appeared on the scene, and Mr.

Staples, the quartermaster, to get the desired information.

At this time the boat became enveloped in steam, and everybody appeared panic-stricken except the crew. I at once from my station in the pilothouse ordered everybody to their stations as I realized by the starboard list of the boat that she must be in a sinking condition.

Almost immediately after this Mr. Wyman and the quartermaster reported to me that the *Larchmont* was in a sinking condition and I think told me that it was the request of the chief engineer that I should beach the boat as soon as possible.

I at once proceeded to the pilot house, rang the necessary bells to start the engines ahead, but could receive no response and I turned again to the deck to superintend the clearing away of the boats.

At this time the *Larchmont* had a very heavy starboard list, in fact, I think her freight deck was under water which brought my own boat which was the forward starboard boat quite near the water.

At this time there were no passengers in the vicinity of my boat, and knowing that the only way to save lives in the proper manner was to lower my boat and go around to the other side of the *Larchmont,* I proceeded at once to have my boat lowered into the water and at this time the ones who got into my boat were the only ones that were on my side of the ship, unless some one might have been aft, hidden by the starboard paddlebox. . . . We at once proceeded around the bow of the sinking *Larchmont* to get her port side to be in a position to save life.

The wind and sea, however, prevented Captain McVey's boat from helping those still aboard the *Larchmont.* In fact, it is doubtful if there were many on the *Larchmont* who could be helped by that time. When the captain had launched his lifeboat into the bitterly cold waters of Long Island Sound, five other lifeboats and two life rafts had already left the ship. It is true that one or two shady forms could be discerned through the steam and spray still standing on the deck, but they made no efforts to jump into the boat. All this time the *Larchmont* had been steadily settling in the water; she soon started her final plunge and disappeared into the icy February seas, carrying with her an unknown number of victims. Since it was then two minutes past eleven o'clock, the entire incident covered a period of twelve minutes.

The six lifeboats and the two rafts were now left floating in the rough seas. As the night wore on, the survivors noticed the gleam of a lighthouse beacon far in the distance and rowed for the welcome flash. The icy waves, driven by a wind which at times reached fifty miles an hour, swept over the boats and rafts until every person was coated with freezing spray. Soon stiffened and numbed by the cold, the passengers and crew huddled together, drifting helplessly before the wind.

Block Island was in the direct path of the survivors. Ashore on the island Keeper Elam P. Littlefield of the Sandy Point Lighthouse had been aroused by the barking of his dog, Leo. Getting up to quiet the animal, Littlefield was startled by a knock against the window pane. He pulled open the door, and a boy fell across the threshold, muttering, "More coming, more coming."

It was then five minutes to six in the morning of February 12. After Keeper Littlefield aroused his wife and five children, he telephoned the New Shoreham Lifesaving Station. Two guests at the lighthouse volunteered to help. On the first trip down to the beach Purser Young of the *Larchmont* was brought back.

"The *Larchmont* has gone down, two hundred have perished," Young gasped, as oil was applied to his face. His body was completely encased in ice.

One after another the survivors were brought into the old Sandy Point Lighthouse, until it resembled a hospital. Bedspreads were torn into strips for bandages to be used on frozen arms and legs. The keeper's eldest daughter, Addie Littlefield, took charge of the newcomers. It was a race with death to keep many of the sufferers alive, but only one man, the Turkish fireman of the wrecked vessel, succumbed.

The work of the keeper was made easier by the arrival of the New Shoreham Lifesavers. Keeper Littlefield drove along the beach with his team, stopping here and there while the victims were placed aboard and rushed to the lighthouse.

A lifeboat came through the breakers with only one man still alive. He jumped ashore. Left in the boat were ten dead men, all but one of whom had slowly frozen to death. This man had cut his own throat to end his agony. The survivor was quickly taken to the lighthouse and cared for. After the living had been attended to, thirty-eight bodies were brought to the station. The young boy, Fred Heirgsell, now began to tell his story of the disaster, and it chilled the hearts of the keeper and his family. He described how the others had frozen to death. According to his account, he, too, was about to fall asleep when the lifeboat grated on the shore. He managed to get out of the lifeboat and started walking along the beach. He was barely able to reach the lighthouse when he was encouraged by the barking of the dog, whose commotion had already aroused the lighthouse keeper. Summoning his remaining strength, Heirgsell rapped on the window pane, and the last he remembered was falling across the open doorway. Others gave equally harrowing tales of exposure and suffering.

Captain McVey landed at Block Island around six thirty that morning, with his hands and feet terribly frozen. He was later taken home to Providence, where he was placed under a doctor's care. Although it had been a bitter experience, he was later subjected to much criticism for his actions. But it is always easy to criticize in times of extreme trouble and danger, and the majority of the sea captains with whom I have talked have believed he did what they would have done.

The schooner *Harry Knowlton,* after striking the *Larchmont,* was abandoned by her captain, Frank T. Haley, and his crew three miles from Block Island. They rowed to safety at the Lifesaving Station of Weekahaug. A prominent Rockland, Maine, sea captain, John I. Snow, later gave me his opinion of the cause of the disaster:

I have talked with both captains, and feel that it was a case of stubbornness on the part of the schooner's captain. According to his sworn testimony Captain Haley saw the steamer's lights less than one hundred yards away from him, but he told his helmsman to keep her on her course. Technically he was right, as a schooner does have the right of way, but it was a case of bullheadedness as the *Knowlton* was yawing considerably.

The disaster which befell the *Larchmont* was the last major marine calamity in the vicinity.

WRECKS IN ATLANTIC WATERS

⚓

PART III

WRECKS IN ATLANTIC WATERS

CHAPTER TEN

The *Phoenix*

What has been the worst hurricane since the Pilgrims landed at Plymouth in 1620 has often been debated by weather historians, but it is now agreed that the title should go to the great hurricane which roared up through the West Indies in the year 1780. This furious gale came right after another terrible tempest which has been remembered with vividness through the years because of a great shipwreck, that of the *Phoenix*. The gale which wrecked the *Phoenix* began on October 3, 1780, preceding the great hurricane by one week.

The first storm had become known as the Savanna-la-Mar * hurricane, and it brought great devastation to much of Jamaica. It struck the island shortly before sunrise on October 3, and the residents went down to the shore to watch the waves roll in. By noon, however, gigantic seas began to form.

* Savanna-la-Mar is located on the west coast of Jamaica.

The waves grew higher and higher until they inundated the beach and rushed half a mile inland! When the storm ended not the slightest trace of man or beast remained, and one entire plantation having forty-two residents was wiped out.*

The *Phoenix* was under the command of Sir Hyde Parker of the Royal Navy, whose career included sea attacks on New York City and Savannah, Georgia. Sir Hyde † had as his first in command a Lieutenant Archer, whose letter to his mother after the disaster has become a classic, parts of which are quoted here:

My dearest Madam,

I am now going to give you an account of our last cruise in the *Phoenix;* and must promise that, should any one see it beside yourself, they must put this construction on it—that it was originally intended for the eyes of a mother, and a mother only—as upon that supposition my feelings may be tolerated. You will also meet with a number of sea terms which if you do not understand, why, I cannot help you, as I am unable to give a sea description in any other words. . . .

On September 30th, weighed; bound for Port Royal, round the eastward of the island. The *Barbadoes* and *Victor* had sailed the day before, and the *Scarborough* was to sail the next. Moderate weather until October 2nd. Spoke to the *Bardadoes,* off Port Antonio, in the evening. At eleven at night it began to snuffle,** with a monstrous heavy bill †† from the eastward. Close-reefed the topsails. Sir Hyde sent for me: "What sort of weather have we, Archer?"

---

* Other craft in addition to the *Phoenix* lost in the same storm were the *Thunderer,* seventy-four-gun man-of-war; *Sterling Castle,* sixty-four guns; and *La Blanche,* forty-two; the *Laurel,* the *Andromeda,* the *Deal Castle,* the *Scarborough,* the *Beaver's Prize,* the *Barbadoes,* the *Cameleon,* the *Endeavor* and the *Victor.*

† Sir Hyde, as he was called, once had Lord Nelson serving under his command.

** To blow in fitful gusts.

†† A chop.

"It blows a little and has a very ugly look. If any other quarter but this, I should say we were going to have a gale of wind."

"Ay, it looks so very often here when there is no wind at all. However, don't hoist the topsails till it clears a little, there is no trusting any country."

At twelve I was relieved. The weather had the same rough look. However, they made sail upon her but had a very dirty night. At eight in the morning I came up again, found it blowing hard from the ENE with close-reefed topsails upon the ship and heavy squalls at times. Sir Hyde came upon deck. "Well, Archer, what do you think of it?"

"O, sir, 'tis only a touch of the times. We shall have an observation at twelve o'clock. The clouds are beginning to break. It will clear up at noon or else blow very hard afterward."

"I wish it would clear up, but I doubt it much. I was once in a hurricane in the East Indies, and the beginning of it had much the same appearance as this. So take in the topsails, we have plenty of searoom.*

At twelve the gale still increasing, we wore ship,† to keep as near midchannel between Jamaica and Cuba as possible. At one the gale increasing still. At two harder! Reefed the courses and furled them. Brought to under a mizzen staysail, head to the northward. In the evening no sign of the weather taking off, but every appearance of the storm increasing. Prepared for a proper gale of wind. Secured all the sails with spare gaskets. Good rolling tackles upon the yards. Squared the booms. Saw the boats all made fast. Now lashed the guns. Double-breeched the lower deckers. Saw that the carpenters had the tarpaulins and battens ** all ready for hatchways. Got

---

* Searoom is space at sea free from obstruction in which a ship can be maneuvered easily.

† To wear ship is to come around on the other tack by turning the head away from the wind. It is the opposite to tacking.

** Battens are strips used to fasten down the edges of the tarpaulin fixed over the hatchways.

the topgallants mast down upon the deck. Jibboom and sprit-sail yard fore and aft. In fact everything we could think of to make a snug ship.

The poor devils of birds now began to find the uproar in the elements, for numbers both of sea and land kinds came on board of us. I took notice of some, which happening to be leeward turned to windward like a ship, back and tack, for they could not fly against it. When they came over the ship they dashed themselves down upon the deck, without attempting to stir till picked up; and when let go again they would not leave the ship, but endeavored to hide themselves from the wind.

At eight o'clock a hurricane. The sea roaring, but the wind still steady to a point. Did not ship a spoonful of water. However, got the hatchways all secured, expecting what would be the consequence should the wind shift. Placed the carpenters by the mainmast with broad axes, knowing from experience that at the moment you may want to cut it away to save the ship an ax may not be found. Went to supper. Bread, cheese and porter.

The purser frightened out of his wits about his bread bags. The two marine officers as white as sheets, not understanding the ship's working so much; and the noise of the lower-deck guns, which by this time made a pretty screeching to the people not used to it. Wooden, our carpenter, was all this time smoking his pipe and laughing at the doctor. The second lieutenant upon deck and the third in his hammock.

At ten o'clock I thought to get a little sleep. Came to look in my cot. It was full of water, for every seam, by the straining of the ship, had begun to leak. Stretched myself, therefore, upon deck between two chests, and left orders to be called should the least thing happen. At twelve a midshipman came to me. "Mr. Archer, we are just going to wear ship, sir."

"O, very well, I'll be up directly. What sort of weather have you got?"

"It blows a hurricane."

Went upon deck, found Sir Hyde there. "It blows hard, Archer."

"It does indeed, sir."

"I don't know that I ever remember its blowing so hard before. But the ship makes a very good weather of it upon this tack; but we must wear her, as the wind has shifted to the SE and we were drawing right upon Cuba. So do you go forward and have some hands stand by. Loose the lee yardarm of the foresail, then when she is right before the wind, whip the clew garnet * close up and roll up the sail."

"Sir, there is no canvas can stand against this a moment. If we attempt to loose him he will fly into ribbons in an instant and we may lose three or four of our people. She'll wear by manning the foreshrouds." †

"O, I don't think she will."

"I'll answer for it, sir. I have seen it tried several times on the coast of America with success."

"Well, try it. If she does not wear we can only loose the foresail afterward."

This was a great condescension from such a man as Sir Hyde. However, by sending about two hundred people into the forerigging, after a hard struggle she wore. Found she did not make so good weather on this tack as on the other, for as the sea began to run across she had not time to rise from one sea before another dashed against her. Began to think we should lose our masts, as the ship lay very much along by the pressure of the wind constantly upon the yards and masts alone. For the poor mizzenstaysail had gone into shreds long before and the sails began to fly from the yards through the gaskets into coach whips. My God! to think that the wind could have such force.

Sir Hyde now sent me to see what was the matter between decks, as there was a great deal of noise. As soon as I was be-

* Clew garnet—a tackle wove through a garnet block.

† A set of ropes leading from the head of a mast, part of the standing rigging.

low, one of the marine officers calls out, "Good God, Mr. Archer, we are sinking! The water is up to the bottom of my cot."

"Pooh, pooh! As long as it is not over your mouth you are well off. What the devil do you make so much noise for?"

I found there was some water between decks but nothing to be alarmed at. Found she made a good deal of water through the sides and decks. Turned the watch below to the pumps, though only two feet of water in the well; but expected to be kept constantly at work now, as the ship labored much, with scarcely a part of her above water but the quarterdeck, and that but seldom. "Come, pump away, my boys. Carpenters, get the weather chain pump rigged."

"All ready, sir."

"Then man it, and keep both pumps going."

At two o'clock the chain pump being choked, we set the carpenters at work to clear it, the two head pumps at work upon deck. The water gained upon us while our chain pumps were idle. In a quarter of an hour they were at work again and we began to gain upon it. While I was standing at the pumps cheering the people the carpenter's mate came running to me with a face as long as my arm. "O, sir! The ship has sprung a leak in the gunner's room."

"Go, then, and tell the carpenter to come to me, but do not speak a word to any one else. . . . Mr. Goodinoh, I am told there is a leak in the gunner's room. Go and see what is the matter but do not alarm anybody, and come and make your report privately to me."

In a short time he returned. "Sir, there is nothing there. It is only the water washing up between the timbers that this booby has taken for a leak."

"O, very well. Go upon deck and see if you can keep any of the water from washing down below."

"Sir, I have four people constantly keeping the hatchways secure, but there is such a weight of water upon the deck that nobody can stand when the ship rolls."

Captain Morton's ship is wrecked on Shag Rocks, Boston Harbor, December 4, 1768, taking with her a treasure chest which has never been found. (*ch. 1*)

Dorothy Snow holds a bone of an elephant drowned in the sinking of the circus ship *Royal Tar*. (*ch. 2*)

The sinking of the *Central America* off Cape Hatteras with a rich cargo of treasure. *(ch. 3)*

The crew of the pinnace *Watch and Wait* cut away the anchor as they are wrecked on the shores of Thacher's Island in August, 1635. (*ch. 4*)

The loss of His Majesty's Ship *Phoenix* in an Atlantic gale, October, 1780. (*ch. 10*)

The Indiaman *Kent* is destroyed by fire, February 28, 1827. (*ch. 12*)

Survivors of the ship *Kent* watch the last moments of their burning vessel. (*ch. 12*)

The East India Company's ship *Doddington* is wrecked off the South African coast. (*ch. 17*)

Survivors of the East Indiaman *Doddington* stranded on a South African island, July 17, 1755. (*ch.* 17)

Shipwreck of the *Jonge Thomas*, a Dutch East Indiaman, on the Cape of Good Hope, Whit-monday, 1773. (*ch.* 19)

Castaways put off on rafts from the wreck of the East Indiaman *Winterton* along the coast of Mozambique, August, 1792. (*ch. 20*)

The *Fanny* is wrecked off the Chinese coast in November, 1803. (*ch.* 21)

The sinking of the *Royal George* as she was being careened off Spithead, August 14, 1782. From a watercolor by Thomas Butterworth. (*ch. 22*)

National Maritime Museum

Removal of the wreckage of the *Royal George* from the floor of the Spithead anchorage. (*ch. 22*)

The steamer *Killarney* is wrecked off the Irish coast in January, 1838. (*ch. 25*)

Survivors of the *Vryheid* in a vain attempt to reach shore lashed to a chicken coop, November, 1802. *(ch. 25)*

The gunner soon afterward came to me saying, "Mr. Archer, I should be glad to have you step this way into the magazine for a moment." I thought some damned thing was the matter, and ran directly. "Well, what is the matter here?" He answered, "The ground tier of the powder is spoiled and I want to show you that it is not out of carelessness in me stowing it, for no powder in the world could be better stowed. Now, sir, what am I to do? If you do not speak to Sir Hyde, he will be angry with me." I could not forbear smiling to see how easy he took the danger of the ship, and said to him, "Let us shake off this gale of wind first and talk of the damaged powder afterward."

At four we gained upon the ship a little and I went upon deck, it being my watch. The second lieutenant relieved me at the pumps. Who can attempt to describe the appearance of things upon deck? If I was to write forever I could not give you an idea of it—a total darkness all above; the sea on fire, running as if it were in the Alps, or Peaks of Teneriffe * (mountains are too common an idea); the wind roaring louder than thunder (absolutely no flight of imagination); the whole made more terrible, if possible, by a very uncommon kind of blue lightning; the poor ship very much pressed, yet doing what she could, shaking her sides and groaning at every stroke. Sir Hyde upon deck lashed to windward! I soon lashed myself alongside of him and told him the situation of things below, saying the ship did not make more water than might be expected in such weather and that I was only afraid of a gun breaking loose. "I am not in the least afraid of that," he said. "I have commanded her six years and have many a gale of wind in her. So that her ironwork, which always gives way first, is pretty well tried. Hold fast! That was an ugly sea. We must lower the yards, I believe Archer. The ship is much pressed."

"If we attempt it, sir, we shall lose them, for a man can do nothing. Besides, their being down would ease the ship very

* Teneriffe, largest of the Canary Islands.

little. The mainmast is a sprung mast. I wish it was overboard without carrying any thing else along with it but that can soon be done, the gale cannot last for ever; 'twill soon be daylight now."

Found by the master's watch that it was five o'clock, though but a little after four by ours. I was glad it was so near daylight and looked for it with much anxiety. Cuba, thou art much in our way! Another ugly sea. Sent a midshipman to bring news from the pumps. The ship was gaining on them very much, for they had broken one of their chains, but it was almost mended again. News from the pump again. "She still gains! A heavy lee!" Backwater from leeward, halfway up the quarterdeck. Filled one of the cutters upon the booms and tore her all to pieces, the ship lying almost on her beam ends and not attempting to right again. Word from below that the ship gained on them, as they could not stand to the pumps, she lay so much along. I said to Sir Hyde: "This is no time, sir, to think of saving the masts. Shall we cut the mainmast away?"

"Ay, as fast as you can."

I accordingly went into the weather chains with a pole-ax, to cut away the lanyards. The boatswain went to leeward and the carpenters stood by the masts. We were all ready, when a violent sea broke right on board of us, carried everything upon deck away, filled the ship with water, the main mizzen-mast went, the ship righted, but was in the last struggle of sinking under us.

As soon as we could shake our heads above water, Sir Hyde exclaimed: "We are gone at last, Archer! Foundered at sea!"

"Yes, sir, farewell, and the Lord have mercy upon us!"

I turned then about to look at the ship and thought she was struggling to get rid of some of the water but all in vain, she was almost full below. "Almighty God! I thank thee, that now I am leaving this world, which I have always considered as only a passage to a better. I die with a full hope of the mercies through the merits of Jesus Christ, thy Son, our Savior!"

I then felt sorry that I could swim, as by that means I might be a quarter of an hour longer dying than a man who could not, and it is impossible to divest ourselves of a wish to preserve life. At the end of these reflections I thought I heard the ship thump and grind under our feet. It was so. "Sir, the ship is ashore!"

"What do you say?"

"The ship is ashore, and we may save ourselves yet!"

By this time the quarterdeck was full of men who had come up from below; and the "Lord have mercy upon us" flying about from all quarters. The ship now made everybody sensible that she was ashore, for every stroke threatened a total dissolution of her whole frame. We found she was stern ashore, and the bow broke the sea a good deal, though it was washing clean over at every stroke. Sir Hyde cried out, "Keep to the quarterdeck, my lads! When she goes to pieces it is your best chance!" Providentially got the foremast cut away, that she might not pay round broadside. Lost five in cutting away the foremast, by the breaking of a sea on board just as the mast went. That was nothing. Everyone expected it would be his own fate next. Looked for daybreak with the greatest impatience. At last it came, but what a scene did it show us! The ship upon a bed of rocks, mountains of them on one side, and Cordilleras * of water on the other. Our poor ship grinding and crying out at every stroke between them, going away by piecemeal. However, to show the unaccountable works of Providence, that which often appears to be the greatest evil proves to be the greatest good. That unmerciful sea lifted and beat us up so high among the rocks that at last the ship scarcely moved. She was very strong and did not go in pieces at the first thumping, though her decks tumbled in. We found afterward that she had beat over a ledge of rocks almost a quarter of a mile in extent beyond us, where if she had struck, every soul of us must have perished.

I now began to think of getting on shore, so I stripped off

* Cordilleras, a Spanish term for a range or chain of mountains.

my coat and shoes for a swim, and looked for a line to carry the end with me. Luckily I could not find one, which gave me time for recollection. "This won't do for me, to be the first man out of the ship, and first lieutenant. We may get to England again and people may think I paid a great deal of attention to myself and did not care for anybody else. No, that won't do. Instead of being the first I'll see every man, sick and well, out of her before me."

I now thought there was no probability of the ship's going to pieces, therefore had not a thought of instant death. Took a look around with a kind of philosophic eye, to see how the same situation affected my companions and was surprised to find the most swaggering, swearing bullies in fine weather now the most pitiful wretches on earth, when death appeared before them. However, two got safe; by which means, with a line, we got a hawser on shore and made fast to the rocks, upon which many ventured and arrived safe. There were some sick and wounded on board, who could not avail themselves of this method. We therefore got a spare topsail yard from the chains and placed one end ashore and the other on the cabin window, so that most of the sick got ashore this way.

As I had determined, so I was the last man out of the ship. This was about ten o'clock. The gale now began to break. Sir Hyde came to me and, taking me by the hand, was so affected that he scarcely was able to speak. "Archer, I am happy beyond expression to see you on the shore, but look at our poor *Phoenix!*" I turned about, but could not say a single word, being too full. My mind had been too intensely occupied before.

By twelve it was pretty moderate. Got some sails on shore and made tents. We found great quantities of fish driven up by the sea into holes of the rocks. Knocked up a fire and had a most comfortable dinner. In the afternoon we made a stage from the cabin windows to the rocks and got out some provisions and water, lest the ship should go to pieces, in which case we must all have perished of hunger and thirst. For we were upon a desolate part of the coast and under a rocky mountain that could not supply us with a single drop of water.

Slept comfortably this night, and the next day the idea of death vanishing by degrees, the prospect of being prisoners during the war, at Havana, and walking three hundred miles to it through the woods, was rather unpleasant. However, to save life for the present we employed this day in getting more provisions and water on shore, which was not an easy matter, on account of decks, guns and rubbish and ten feet of water that lay over them. In the evening I proposed to Sir Hyde to repair the remains of the only boat left and to venture in her to Jamaica myself. And, in case I arrived safe, to bring vessels to take them all off. A proposal worthy of consideration. It was next day agreed to. Therefore we got the cutter on shore and set the carpenters to work on her.

In two days she was ready and at four o'clock in the afternoon I embarked with four volunteers and a fortnight's provisions. Hoisted English colors as we put off from shore, and received three cheers from the lads left behind, and set sail with a light heart, having not the least doubt that, with God's assistance, we should come and bring them all off. Had a very squally night and a very leaky boat, so as to keep two buckets constantly bailing. Steered her myself the whole night by the stars and in the morning saw the coast of Jamaica, distant twelve leagues. At eight in evening arrived at Montego Bay.

I must now begin to leave off, particularly as I have but half an hour to conclude. Else my pretty little short letter will lose its passage, which I should not like after being ten days, at different times, writing it, beating up with the convoy to the northward, which is a reason that this epistle will never read well. For I never sat down with a proper disposition to go on with it. But as I knew something of the kind would please you, I was resolved to finish it. Yet it will not bear an overhaul, so do not expose your son's nonsense.

But to proceed—I instantly sent off an express to the Admiral, another to the *Porcupine* man of war, and went myself to Martha Bray to get vessels. Got three small vessels and set out back again to Cuba, where I arrived the fourth day after leaving my companions. I thought the ship's crew would have devoured me on my landing. They presently whisked me up on their shoulders and carried me to the tent where Sir Hyde was.

I must omit little occurrences that happened on shore, for want of time, but I shall have a number of stories to tell when I get alongside of you.

I found the *Porcupine* had arrived that day and the lads had built a boat almost ready for launching that would hold fifty of them, was intended for another trial, in case I had foundered. Next day embarked all our people that were left, amounting to two hundred and fifty. For some had died of the wounds they received in getting on shore, others of drinking rum, and others had straggled into the country. All our vessels were so full of people that we could not take away the few clothes that were saved from the wreck, but that was a trifle since we had preserved our lives and liberty. To make short my story, we all arrived safe at Montego Bay and shortly after at Port Royal—in the *Janus* which was sent on purpose for us, and were all honorably acquitted for the loss of the ship. Found that in my absence I had been appointed captain of the *Tobago*, where I remain His Majesty's most true and faithful servant, and my dear mother's most dutiful son,

ARCHER.

CHAPTER ELEVEN

The *Atalante*

⚓

On the morning of the tenth of November, 1813, the ship *Atalante* under command of Captain Frederick Hickey, stood in for Halifax Harbor, Nova Scotia, during very foggy weather. The men were carefully sounding their way with the lead, and there were lookouts everywhere trying to catch a glimpse of land.

After breakfast, a fog signal-gun was fired in the expectation of its being answered by the lighthouse on Cape Sambro,* near which it was known the ship must be. Within a few minutes, a gun was heard in the north northwest quarter, exactly where the light was believed to lie. As the soundings agreed with the estimated position of the ship, and as the guns from the *Atalante,* fired at intervals of fifteen minutes, were

* In 1873 another ship, the *Atlantic,* her master Captain Williams, also made an error in regard to Sambro Light, and 481 of the 931 aboard were drowned. See my *Great Gales and Dire Disasters.*

regularly answered in the direction of the harbor's mouth, it was determined to attempt to enter the port under the guidance of these sounds alone.

By a fatal coincidence, the answering guns were fired, not by Cape Sambro Lighthouse, but by H.M.S. *Barrossa,* which was likewise entangled with the fog. She, too, supposed that she was communicating with the lighthouse, whereas it was the guns of the unfortunate *Atalante* that she heard all the time.

There was a risk incurred by running in for Halifax Harbor under such circumstances even if the guns had been fired by the lighthouse, but it often becomes an officer's duty to put his ship, as well as his life, in hazard; and this appears to have been one of those unfortunate cases.

Captain Hickey had urgent dispatches aboard concerning the enemy's fleet, and there was every appearance that the fog would last a week. As the captain had passed over the ground a hundred times before, it was decided to try to make port, and the ship was steered in the supposed direction of Halifax.

They had not stood on for long before one of the lookouts shouted, "Breakers ahead! Hard a-starboard!" But it was too late. Before the helm could be put over, the ship was amongst the terrible Sister's Rocks, located on the eastern ledge of Sambro Island.

The rudder and half of the sternpost, together with a great part of the false keel, were driven off at the first blow, and soon floated up alongside. There is some reason to believe that a portion of the bottom of the ship, loaded with 120 tons of iron ballast, was torn from the upper works by this fearful blow and that the hull, which instantly filled with water, was afterward buoyed up merely by the empty casks.

The captain now ordered the guns to be thrown overboard; but before one of them could be cast loose, or a breeching cut, the great ship went over on her beam ends. Several of the guns were fired as signals of distress, but none could now be thrown over.

The quarter boats were then lowered into the water with some difficulty; but the jolly boat, which happened to be on the poop * undergoing repairs, struck against one of the stern davits, bilged † and went down. As the ship was now falling fast over on her beam ends, directions were given to cut away the fore and main masts. Fortunately, they fell without injuring the large boat on the booms—their one last hope. At the instant of this crash, the ship parted in two between the main and mizzen masts. The poor *Atalante* was now divided into three pieces, crumbling into smaller fragments at every new billow.

By this time a great number of the men had scrambled into the pinnace ** on the booms, in hopes that she might float off as the ship sank. Captain Hickey, however, realizing that the boat would sink at once, ordered twenty of the men to quit her. His orders were promptly obeyed.

Throughout the whole of these trying moments the discipline of the ship was maintained with a great degree of cheerfulness. Even when the masts fell, the sound of the crashing spars was drowned in the shouts of the crew, though they were clinging to the weather gunwale. The sea, from time to time, made a clean breech over them.

As soon as the pinnace was relieved from the pressure of the men, she was knocked off by a wave, which turned her bottom upward and pushed her into the surf amidst the fragments of the wreck. The sailors plunged into the sea and succeeded in righting the boat after a great struggle. They slid in over the gunwales, bailed for some time and then waited for

* The stern's highest deck.
† When a ship is bilged her bottom is stove in.
** A small, light vessel, first used in 1546 and usually employed as a tender.

further orders. The captain, with about forty men, still clung to the remains of the *Atalante*.

An attempt was next made to construct a raft, as it was feared the three boats could not possibly carry all hands, but the violence of the waves prevented this. It now was absolutely necessary, however, to take the crew off the wreck, which was disappearing rapidly. Most of the men got aboard the pinnace, where they were laid flat on the bottom, like herring in a barrel. Then the small boats returned to pick off the rest. This proved no easy matter, and in several cases it was found impossible. As a result many men had to swim for it, while others were dragged through the waves by ropes.

Amongst the crew there was one fellow, a Negro fiddler, who was discovered clinging to the main chains, with his beloved Cremona * violin squeezed tightly but delicately, under his arm. Even at this moment, with the threat of death all around them, the sailors could not refrain from making a joke of the Negro's situation, for he must lose one of two things—his fiddle or his life. So, at last, after a painful struggle, the man and his violin were obliged to part company, and he dropped the precious instrument into the sea.

Another laugh was at the expense of the captain's clerk. This zealous person had general instructions that whenever guns were fired, or any other circumstance occurred likely to shake the chronometer, he was to hold it in his hand, to prevent further concussion deranging its works. Therefore, as soon as the ship dashed against the rocks, the clerk's thoughts naturally turned to the timepiece. He caught it up and ran on deck. Being no swimmer, he clung to the mizzenmast, forgetting everything but his important trust.

When the ship fell over, the mast became nearly horizontal, and the clerk managed to creep along till he reached the

* A town in Lombardy famous for violins.

mizzentop, where he seated himself, grinning like a monkey with a coconut. Then the spar gave way, and he was plunged, chronometer and all, down into the sea! Every eye was now turned to the spot, to see whether he would ever appear again. Then, to the joy of all hands, he emerged from the waves, the chronometer still in hand! It was with great difficulty that he and his charge were finally dragged into the boat. Everything else on board, except the admiral's precious dispatches, was lost.

The pinnace now contained seventy-nine men and one woman, the cutter forty-two men and the gig eighteen. With such overloading they barely floated. Captain Hickey, in the true tradition of the sea, was the last man to leave the wreck.

So speedy, indeed, was the work of destruction that by the time the captain reached the boat, the *Atalante* had almost entirely "melted into the yeast of waves." As she went down, the crew gave her three hearty cheers, and then finally abandoned the scattered fragments of what had been their house and home for nearly seven years.

The fog still continued as thick as ever, and the survivors were without a compass. The wind was still light and there was great difficulty in steering a straight course.

At this moment of greatest need, an old quartermaster, Samuel Shanks by name, recollected that he carried at the end of his watch chain a small compass-seal. This precious discovery was announced to the other boats by a joyous shout from the pinnace, and the compass was speedily handed to the captain in the gig, where it was placed on the top of the chronometer. The little needle remained sufficiently steady for steering the boats within a few points. Thus they were assured of hitting land.

The survivors soon fell in with an old fisherman, who piloted them the remainder of the distance to a bight called

Portuguese Cove, where they all landed in safety. They now found they were twenty miles from Halifax.

The fishermen lighted great fires to warm their shivering guests, most of whom were thinly clad, and all of them dripping wet.* Those who had entered the boats last and were forced to swim for their lives had thrown off everything but their trousers, and it turned out that the only decently dressed person out of the whole party was old Shanks, the owner of the watch and compass-seal. Shanks was a real hard-weather sailor, who took the whole affair as deliberately as if shipwreck had been an everyday occurrence. He did not even take off his hat, except, indeed, to give his good ship a cheer as she went to the bottom.

The captain guided the three boats round to the harbor, taking with him the men who had suffered most fatigue, and those who were worst off for clothes. The officers then set out with the rest to march across the country to Halifax. Very few of the party wore shoes. There was not a single straggler, however, and the whole ship's company, officers, men and boys, assembled in the evening at Halifax, in as orderly a manner as if their ship had met with no accident.

It is highly important to notice that the lives of the crew could not have been saved had the excellent discipline not prevailed. Had any impatience been shown to rush the boats, or had the captain not possessed sufficient authority to make the men leave the overcrowded pinnace, at least half of the crew must have lost their lives.

* Here the officers learned that the *Barrossa* had reached port safely.

CHAPTER TWELVE

Loss of the Indiaman *Kent*

One of the classic shipwreck stories of the Atlantic Ocean's history is that of the *Kent,* a fine new vessel, commanded by Captain Henry Cobb. On Saturday, February 19, 1825, she left England, bound for Bengal and China. She had on board a crew of 148 men, with 20 military officers, 344 soldiers, 43 women and 66 children, belonging to the 31st Regiment, as well as 20 private passengers. In all there were 641 persons aboard.

The *Kent* proceeded without incident on her voyage until the night of February 28, when a violent gale sprang up from the west. All the following morning the wind gradually increased. So intense was the storm that by afternoon the main chains of the ship were considerably underwater.

Everything was done to secure the safety of the vessel. In the course of his duty, one of the officers went into the hold, accompanied by two sailors, in order to see that all was fast. They carried with them a patent lantern.

Seeing that the lamp burned dimly, the officer took the precaution to hand it up to the deck to be trimmed. Having discovered that one of the spirit casks had broken loose from its fastenings, he told the sailors to get some billets of wood to secure it. He waited for their return, bracing his left hand against the cask as he held the lighted lamp in his right. While they were gone the ship gave a sudden heavy lurch, and the officer dropped the lamp. At that very moment the cask tore free from his hand. It stove in at once, and the spirits were ignited by the lamp. A few moments later the hold was in flames.

Spreading rapidly the blaze soon sent great volumes of thick smoke to all parts of the *Kent*. "The flames have reached the cable tier!" came the cry, and the strong pitchy smell that reached the deck soon confirmed the truth. With no alternative Captain Cobb ordered the lower decks to be scuttled and the lower portholes of the vessel to be opened, so that the fire might be put out by the inrushing ocean.

These orders were speedily carried out, but several of the unhappy passengers had already perished from suffocation. So dense was the smoke that it was with the greatest difficulty anyone could remain long enough below deck to carry out the captain's wishes. Finally the sea rushed in with extraordinary force. The immense quantity of water checked the fury of the flames for a time, but there was a new source of danger, for the ship was becoming waterlogged and might sink at any moment.

It was a weird scene of horror. The upper deck was covered with between 500 and 600 human beings, many of whom had fled from below absolutely naked, and were now running about in quest of husbands, children or parents. Some were stunned by the situation while others were in frantic despair.

Several were on their knees, earnestly imploring the mercy of God. A number of the older and braver soldiers and sailors took their seats directly over the powder magazine—trusting that the explosion which they expected at any moment might make their end a speedy one.

All hope had now departed. One man was seen removing a lock of hair from his writing desk to his pocket. Another officer wrote a short letter to his father, which he afterward carefully enclosed in a bottle, in the hope that it might eventually reach its destination and solve the mystery of his death.

Fourth Mate Thompson now sent a man aloft to search the horizon for a possible sail. As soon as the sailor reached the foretop he scanned the horizon, and for those below it was a moment of unutterable suspense. Then, waving his hat, the lookout shouted, "Sail, on the lee bow!" The sighting was received with thanksgivings and answered by three loud cheers from those on deck. Signals of distress were instantly hoisted, minute guns fired, and plans made to bear down upon the stranger, which proved to be the *Cambria*, a small brig of two hundred tons commanded by Captain Cook. Bound to Vera Cruz, she had on board twenty Cornish miners.

For ten or fifteen agonizing minutes, those on the *Kent* were in doubt as to whether the brig saw their signals, or if seeing them, would give them any assistance. From the violence of the gale, as they afterward learned, the report of the guns was not heard, but the fire and smoke from the *Kent* had already attracted the attention of those on the *Cambria*. The brig hoisted British colors, and crowded all sail as it hastened to their relief. While the vessel was approaching, arrangements were made for getting out the boats. Before hoisting out the first boat, the sailors filled it with the soldiers' wives and children, who had hurriedly wrapped themselves in whatever articles of clothing they could find. At about half-past two o'clock they had come from the after cabins to the starboard cuddy port, from the outside of which the cutter was suspended. Not a sound was heard, for even the babies stopped crying. In two cases wives begged to be left behind with their husband, but were refused. Finally all were in the boat which was immediately lowered toward the sea.

Every precaution was taken to prevent swamping, with a man stationed at each end with an axe, ready to cut the ropes, in case of trouble in unhooking the boat. The little craft reached the water, the stern tackle was cleared, but the ropes at the bow fouled. Time and again the axe swung against the entangled lines, but to no avail. The boat was soon in danger of hanging perpendicularly by the bow, with the passengers spilling out, but a sudden wave struck the stern and lifted it up, so the seamen cleared the tackle and the boat was free! Soon the oarsmen began pulling toward the brig. In a relatively short time the boat reached the *Cambria* and all passengers were put aboard.

After the first trip, the boats could not come alongside the *Kent,* so a plan was adopted for lowering the women and children by ropes from the stern, two-and-two together. But because of the heaving of the ship and the extreme difficulty of dropping them at the instant the boat was underneath, many of the poor creatures were unavoidably plunged underwater. All the women survived this rough usage, but several children perished in the sea.

Two or three soldiers sprang into the water with their children, and perished in their endeavors to save them. One man, having to choose between losing his wife or his children, decided in favor of his wife, and four children perished. One fine fellow, a soldier, who had neither wife nor child of his own, lashed three children to him. He leaped into the water; but not being able to reach the boat, he was drawn back again into the ship. Two of the children had drowned. One man fell down the hatchway into the flames. Another dropped to his death between the boat and the brig, while some were lost in their attempts to climb the sides of the *Cambria*.

As the day was drawing to a close, a rope was suspended from the extremity of the spanker boom to speed operations. The men were directed to proceed along the boom and slide down by the rope, but the great swells allowed the boats to retain their position for only a moment. Most of the men who adopted this course were either left for a time swinging in midair, plunged into the sea or violently flung against the lifeboat.

At length, when nearly every person was off the ship, and only those who refused to leave were still aboard, Captain Cobb left the ill-fated vessel. After he reached the *Cambria*, he watched as the flames spread along the upper deck of the *Kent*, climbed with the speed of lightning to the masts and rigging to form one general conflagration. The burning ship illuminated the heavens to a great distance for more than an hour. Then the masts, fell like tall church steeples, over the ship's side. It was about one thirty in the morning when the fire reached the powder magazine and the long-expected explosion took place. Everyone watched as fragments of the *Kent* soared into the sky like so many rockets, and then fell back into the sea.

The *Cambria* made all sail to the nearest port, and although the violence of the gale continued, she arrived shortly after midnight on the third of March at Falmouth, where the *Kent* survivors were received with the utmost kindness by the inhabitants.

Wonderful to relate, the flames and explosion had attracted the notice of the crew of another ship, the *Caroline*, on her passage from Alexandria to Liverpool, and she immediately bore down upon the wreck. Fortunately, they were just in time to save twelve persons whom they found floating on a mast. The captain of the *Caroline,* with the greatest humanity, remained in the neighborhood all night, in the hope of assisting any who might have taken refuge on other parts of the wreck. In the morning they rescued two more of the unfortunate survivors, being all whom they could discover, from the floating masses of wreckage. The sky began to assume a stormy aspect, and the boat which had been sent out was forced to return to the ship, which once more proceeded on her voyage. No more survivors were ever found.

CHAPTER THIRTEEN

Eaten by Sharks

The island of Cuba has gone through many rebellions and revolutions since 1826 when the story in this chapter took place, and scores of fiendish deeds have occurred during that long period. In spite of this I am never able to recall without a sensation of horror the account of the sinking of the *Magpie* in Cuban waters more than a century and a quarter ago.

A relatively small schooner, the *Magpie* operated in the Gulf of Mexico under the command of Lieutenant Edward Smith. Carrying a crew of twenty-four, she sailed in search of pirate vessels.

On the night of August 27, 1826, the *Magpie* was anchored near the Colorados Roads off western Cuba, awaiting the possible appearance of a pirate vessel. It was an evening to remember, for the sea breeze had lulled, with a dead calm settling over the silent waters of the Gulf of Mexico.

At sunset Lieutenant Smith climbed to the masthead and

began studying the horizon with his spyglass. He searched for signs of the pirate vessel until dusk, in vain. Coming down from the masthead, he retired to his cabin for the night. Meanwhile, the mate and the crew were out on deck, talking over their former adventures. Everything in the area apparently was in perfect security.

The schooner had her fore-topsail set, with the yard braced for the starboard tack and the foresail in the brails.* The jib and boom mainsail, the latter with the tack triced up, were hanging up and down in the calm.

On the larboard bow a small black cloud hung over the land. Almost always in the tropics when the afternoon clouds begin settling on the hills it is a sign that the land breeze is about to commence. Generally speaking, the land wind comes in light flaws, until it eventually reaches its full strength. The typical sea captain of the period, beating all day against the sea breezes and the current, would welcome the arrival of the evening's fair land wind and cooling breeze which would help him sail toward his destination.

The small black cloud gradually increased in size, and the moon, now shining brightly, made it appear darker than it was in contrast. Looking at the gathering blackness the mate experienced a feeling of approaching trouble which made him uneasy. He decided to warn Lieutenant Smith, and looked down the hatchway into the cabin.

"Mr. Smith," he called, "I think that the land breeze will be coming off rather strong, sir. The clouds now look black."

"Very well," answered his superior officer. "I'll be up on deck in a moment."

Meanwhile the cloud, now swollen to tremendous proportions, appeared to be moving toward the schooner. The crew members who five minutes before had been telling stories

---

* A brail is a rope fastened to the leech or corner of a sail and leading through a block by which the sail can be hauled up or in as in furling.

were now strangely silent. As the cloud approached they did not speak, for there seemed to be a deathlike stillness in the air.

Suddenly, without further warning, a terrific squall of wind and rain hit the *Magpie*. It came so fast that the mate was unable to call the watch, and the schooner began to capsize! At the moment, Lieutenant Smith was putting his foot on the last step of the ladder. He felt the *Magpie* heel over, and was thrown into the water as his schooner sank forever beneath him. The survivors now found themselves in the water. Two of their companions, caught below, had gone to the bottom with the vessel.

Strangely enough, no sooner had the *Magpie* disappeared than the wind stopped blowing, another dead calm set in, and in ten minutes the bright rays of the moon again illuminated the sky. Then there was a commotion in the water. The schooner's longboat, which evidently had broken loose from its position on the booms, broke the surface, but, of course, she was swamped.

All the survivors scrambled into the boat, and she capsized. They attempted to climb on her keel, but since only a few could huddle there, the others clung to her gunwales.*

Lieutenant Smith realized that unless the men turned the boat over and bailed her out many of them would soon drown. He begged them to right the craft and empty her, which the crew instantly did.

Two men slid over the gunwales and began bailing the water out with their hats. They were doing very well when suddenly there was a disturbance in the water. All at once the triangular fin of a shark was seen gliding along about fifty feet away.

"A shark!" shouted one frantic sailor, and in the excite-

* Gunwales are the upper edges of a boat or ship's sides.

ment which followed, over went the boat again and the men were soon fighting for places on the keel. This time, as the shark drew near, the men fought desperately. One would gain temporary possession of the keel and then be dislodged by a frantic companion.

Smith urged the men to kick with their feet in the water. He shouted that sharks would not attack under such conditions. Soon his companions began to calm down again, and they righted the boat, kicking with their feet all the time.

Four men climbed in and all began steady bailing, until they had cleared the longboat of water down to the thwarts. Twenty minutes more would have been enough time to allow all hands to get in. At this moment, however, a great noise was heard a short distance away, and no fewer than fifteen sharks were seen approaching them.

The panic was ten times greater than before, and over went the longboat again. At first the sharks appeared harmless, swimming in among their intended victims and rubbing against the legs of the men. At times, they would leap about, apparently playing in the water. Then came the moment when one man felt sharp teeth against his leg. Suddenly he gave a hopeless scream as he felt his leg completely severed from his body.

No sooner had the blood been tasted, than the dreaded mass attack took place. The sharks swam toward the men, and the air was filled with shrieks as one and then another unfortunate lost a leg.

Some of the crew were torn from the boat, to which they tried to cling; others sank to their death from fear alone. Mr. Smith, treading water as he clung to the gunwales, still gave his orders with clearness and coolness, and the poor men still obeyed. Again the boat was righted, and again two men slid over the gunwales to bail her.

The survivors, as before, clung to the sides and kept the

boat upright. Mr. Smith, himself, held by the stern and cheered and applauded his men. But the sharks had tasted blood, and were not to be driven from their feast. In one brief moment, when Mr. Smith rested from his splashing and looked into the boat to watch its progress, a giant shark swished toward him, seized his legs and bit both of them off just above the knees. Human nature was not strong enough to bear the immense pain without a groan, and it was deep and audible. The crew had long respected their gallant commander; they knew his worth and his courage. Two of them grasped their dying officer and placed him in the stern sheets.

Even now, in agony, Smith forgot his own sufferings, and thought only of rescuing the remaining few. He gave them a message, and concluded by saying, "If any of you survive this fatal night, and return to Jamaica, tell the admiral [Sir Laurence Halsted] that I was in search of the pirate when this lamentable occurrence took place; tell him I hope I have always done my duty, and that I—" here the endeavor of some of the men to get into the boat gave her a heel to one side; those who were supporting Smith relinquished him for a moment, and he rolled overboard and was drowned. His last bubbling cry was soon lost amidst the shrieks of his former companions—he sank into the ocean and was seen no more.

With him died every hope. All but two of the crew gave way to loud cries of grief and cursings. Some, who had not been seriously injured by the monsters of the deep, endeavored to get upon the keel of the boat, which had again upset.

By now, however, they were exhausted from their struggles, and soon gave up the unequal fight, not caring when or how they met death. They either were eaten immediately by the sharks or, courting death, threw themselves from their only support and were drowned. The last to perish was a sailor named Wilson, to whom Lieutenant Smith had given the message to be delivered to Admiral Halsted.

Finally there were only two survivors, Jack Maclean and Tom Meldrum. It had been eight o'clock in the evening when the *Magpie* upset, and the two men later figured that their companions had all died by nine. The sharks seemed satisfied for the time being. Jack and Tom, who had been clutching the keel, seized the interlude to right the boat.

Maclean climbed in over the bows and Meldrum over the stern. Still alive and in comparative security, they began to bail again. Aftr twenty minutes of hard work they had lightened the boat. Then both sat down to rest, exhausted. A short time later the sharks returned. The creatures endeavored to upset the boat, swimming along and bumping it time and again. After circling the craft for a while, they departed, and the two seamen found themselves free for the moment.

Tired as they were, the men continued to bail until the boat was nearly dry. Then both lay down to rest again, one forward and the other aft. They soon fell into a sound sleep, and day dawned before they awoke to horrible reality. The sun rose clear and unclouded, the cool of the night was followed by the sultry calm of the morning. Heat, hunger, thirst and fatigue settled on the unfortunate survivors.

They looked out across the water as far as they could see, but no object was in sight. An endless ocean, a cloudless sky and a fiercely burning sun were all they had to gaze upon. The boat lay in a world alone! They had no oar, no mast, no sail—nothing but the bare planks and themselves, without provisions or water. They settled themselves under the thwarts, or seats, hopeless, friendless and miserable.

" 'Tis a bad business, this," said Jack Maclean from his position in the bow, "a very bad business, indeed. I am sorry I was not eaten by the sharks with the rest of the poor fellows, and then I should never have known the misery of this moment."

"I have been in many a heavy squall before now," replied Tom Meldrum, "but I never felt such a fix as this—no hope, Jack, none! Here we are, doomed to die of thirst and hunger! —nothing to eat, nothing."

They looked at each other, wondering what the outcome would be when their need of food would overwhelm their sanity. The same thoughts then entered the mind of each— that if no ship passed within twenty-four hours, it was possible that one might murder the other for food!

It was now half-past six in the morning. The sun was beginning to burn through, and the sea was as smooth as a looking glass. All was calm and hushed. In vain the two sailors strained their eyes, in vain they turned from side to side to escape the burning rays of the sun. They could not sleep, for now anxiety and fear of the other kept each vigilant.

Complaining of terrible thirst Maclean often dipped his hand into the water to suck the fluid. As he did so, not infrequently the sharp fin of a shark was seen close to the boat.

Then came the dramatic moment that morning when Meldrum, scanning the sea, saw a white sail on the horizon.

"By God, there is a sail!" he called out.

The two men jumped into each other's arms and soon were laughing and crying together. Indeed, it was a sail. A brig had a light breeze aloft and was steering exactly in their direction. Meldrum stood up on the thwart and flung his jacket high in the air, while Maclean, although the stranger was miles distant, endeavored to hail her. Sometimes they shouted together, in order to produce a louder sound, and occasionally both stood up to make some signal. They kept watching the brig, and forgot everything—the burning sun, and their hunger and thirst.

Suddenly, as they watched, the vessel swung around three points * and started on a tack which would take her on a parallel course to their boat, probably too far away to be sure to see the unhappy seamen.

In vain they hailed, in vain they threw their jackets in the air, for they were not seen, and the brig continued on her new course. They now tried to break off a thwart, or seat, to paddle with, but failed. Then they attempted to heel, or tip, the boat and paddle by hand, but they soon realized as they paddled that it made it harder for them to be seen, and so finally stopped. They watched a man going aloft on the brig. Seeing him distinctly, they shouted and waved their jackets. The man paid them no attention.

Time was slipping away. If once they got abaft the beam of the brig, every second would lessen the chance of being seen. Then it was that Meldrum looked first at the brig, then at his companion.

"By heaven, I'll do it, or we are lost!"

"Do what?"

"I'll tell you, Jack, that I'll swim to her; if I get safe to her, you are safe."

"What! jump overboard, and leave me all alone?" replied Maclean. "Look at that shark, which has followed us all night. Why, it is only waiting for you to get into the water to swallow you. No, no—wait, wait, perhaps another vessel may come!"

Both men watched the fin of the shark move through the water about twenty yards from the boat. Now and then another and another could be seen. Death surely awaited them in the boat, only less possibly so in the sea.

"Well," said Tom finally, "if we wait we must die, and if I get to the brig, we will be saved. If the sharks come, God will

* A point is 7½ degrees of the compass, originally known as 1/12 of a quadrant.

protect me! Good-bye—now if you see those devils in chase
of me, splash or make some noise to frighten them, but don't
tell me you see them coming. God bless you, Jack. Keep your
eye upon me, and keep making signals to the brig."

He fell on his knees and said, "God protect me!" Meldrum
then jumped overboard with as much calmness as if he were
merely taking a swim. Maclean cheered his companion,
looked across at the oncoming brig and wildly waved his
jacket. Then he turned to watch the sharks. He soon saw
three monsters swim past the boat in the direction of his
companion! He splashed his jacket in the water to scare them
away, but they lazily pursued their course.

Meldrum was still swimming strongly. There was no doubt
that he would pass within hail of the brig provided the sharks
did not get him first. He continued to kick the water and
splash as he swam. Then came the chilling moment when
he saw one of the terrifying creatures by his side. Frightened,
he still swam and kicked, but his mind was ready for the
worst, and he had little hope of success.

The wind began to freshen, and the brig was soon running
faster through the water. To Tom Meldrum the sails seemed
bursting with the breeze. Now close enough to hope his voice
might be heard, he hailed and hailed at the top of his lungs.
Not a soul was to be seen on deck except the man at the
wheel, who was too intent upon his course to notice the call.
The brig passed, close to the swimmer, and then every second
increased the distance between them. Hope was gone, and the
swim had exhausted him. The sharks now waited merely for
the first quiet moment to dispose of their victim.

Gunner Meldrum knew a return to the boat was impossible. He realized that in his exhausted condition he never
could have reached her. Just as he began to offer up his last
prayer to God, he saw a man look over the quarter of the brig.
Raising both his hands to attract the man's attention, Mel-

drum began to tread water. Then, to his joy, he saw the flash of a telescope as the man on the quarter-deck aimed it at him. A moment later a boat was let down as the brig was hove to. It was only five minutes afterward that Gunner Tom Meldrum was pulled to safety out of the sea, and the shark gave up and swam away. Ten minutes later Jack Maclean was rescued, and both survivors were soon aboard the brig. They had won their awesome fight with death.

CHAPTER FOURTEEN

Collins, the Good Samaritan

It is an unwritten law of the sea that a vessel able to do so should give aid to any person or ship in distress. In my book *Women of the Sea* I mention Good Samaritans who, to their own subsequent financial loss, stopped to help out vessels in trouble. Often they would be taken to task for delaying their voyage in order to save lives. Fortunately this was not always so, as in the case of Captain John Collins.

The Collins line was started by Edward K. Collins, who was born at Truro, Massachusetts. By 1825, he managed a fleet of packets. In 1836 he started the Dramatic Line and named his vessels after actors—*Roscius, Siddons, Sheridan* and *Garrick.* A smaller ship, the *Shakespeare,* he already owned. Desiring the best sea captains he could find to command these new ships, he looked to Cape Cod for their masters. His own uncle, John Collins of Truro, was the first he chose. He built the *Garrick* and *Sheridan* in 1836, with the *Siddons* coming in 1837. When his flagship, the *Roscius*,* went sliding down the ways in 1839, she was the largest merchantman afloat having a mainmast of 160 feet and a main yard 75 feet long.

Truro-born John Collins gladly became her captain. He had shipped before the mast when he was fifteen, sailed on a blockade runner during the War of 1812 and was captured by the British, after which he was thrown into one of the infamous English prisons. When the war ended he did so well on the *Shakespeare* that he was rewarded with command of the *Roscius*.

Captain John Collins had a long list of rescues at sea to his credit. One of these acts of heroism was the occasion on which he saved the crew of the Truro fishing schooner *Garnet*. During a violent gale his lookout had seen a schooner flying a distress signal. Captain Collins saved all aboard just at the last minute, and then to his surprise found that he had rescued a former fellow townsman of Truro.

For saving the passengers of the English bark *Scotia*, Collins received medals from the Humane Societies of London and Liverpool, while the British government presented him with a silver service and several gold medals for his heroism at sea.

Seldom is it possible for the reader to be given the story of a tragic shipwreck which was written by an observer on the scene at the time. In 1839, when an English ship was hit by a terrible hurricane which left her waterlogged far out on the Atlantic Ocean, circumstances allowed the rescue of her crew and passengers to be described by an eyewitness.

That year of 1839 was distinguished by the number and the severity of the hurricanes which battered the North Atlantic regions. New England suffered three terrible storms in

* Named for a famous Roman actor of more than 2,000 years ago.

the month of December alone, in one of which the *Hesperus* was wrecked in Boston Harbor.*

On the fifth of the same month Captain Collins of the *Roscius* sighted the *Scotia,* far out on the Atlantic in sinking condition. Changing her course, the packet ship came up with the ill-fated craft and stood by. The following is from the pen of Dr. R. R. Madden, a passenger aboard the *Roscius* who watched the entire proceedings from her deck:

Fifth of December, P.M. Fell in with the wreck of the *Scotia,* bound from Quebec to Glasgow, burthen 600 tons, loaded with timber, water-logged, in latitude 46°, longitude 32° 30'. On seeing signals of distress flying, we altered our course and bore down on her; and on the *Roscius* approaching her, Captain Collins hailed her; the answer was, "We are water-logged—seventeen feet water in her hold!" The prompt reply of Captain Collins was, "If you want to come on board, put out your boats."

A cheer from the people of the sinking vessel followed; such a cry as men in desperate circumstances alone could utter; and that thrilling cry went up as the simultaneous shout of men in the extremest peril suddenly restored to life and hope; and instantly every hat and cap was seen waving on the crowded poop.

An effort was now made to approach us, but the water-logged vessel was utterly unmanageable; she pitched heavily, as if she would have gone down headlong; the seas swept over her, and, as she rose, broke through her broken ports. Her mizzen-topmast, and fore and main-topgallantmasts had been cut away to ease her, and the poop-deck, where the crew were congregated, seemed the only place of safety left them.

* Longfellow used this wreck to tell of the "Wreck of the Hesperus," borrowing the name *Hesperus* for his ballad. Actually the craft from which the woman mentioned in the poem washed ashore was the *Favorite* of Wiscasset, Maine, and the incident took place at Cape Ann. I tell the entire story in my *Mysteries and Adventures Along the Atlantic Coast.*

In attempting to near us, she came staggering down on us, and we were compelled to make sail to get out of her way. The sea was very heavy—we again lay to, and were then about a mile from the *Scotia*. Night came on, and no boats were seen—the unfortunate *Scotia* was then lost sight of altogether. About six o'clock, Captain Collins hoisted a lantern, and the light was immediately answered by the *Scotia*. It was the opinion of Captain Collins that one of their boats had put off, and had been swamped in attempting to reach us, and that the survivors had determined to wait till morning before another attempt was made. It seemed, indeed, doubtful, in the extreme, if any small boat could live in such a sea.

It is impossible sufficiently to commend the conduct of Captain Collins;—his anxiety to reach Liverpool before the steamer, which was to have sailed six days after us, made every moment of importance. We had, moreover, seventy steerage passengers, and twenty-one in the cabin; and to forego taking advantage of a fair wind, and to lay to for a night in a heavy sea, with every appearance of an approaching gale, was a determination which, I greatly fear, many a master of a ship would have found great difficulty in coming to.

Captain Collins, however, made this resolution promptly, and without any expression of impatience at the detention it occasioned. His only observation was, "We must stay by the poor devils, at all events, till morning—we can't leave them to perish there, damn it." May we not hope, when the "accusing spirit flew up to heaven's chancery with the oath, and blushed as he gave it in, the recording angel, as he wrote it down, dropped a tear upon the word, and blotted it out forever?"

At seven P.M., cheering was heard in the direction of the *Scotia;* the people, we supposed, had taken the boats, and had then left the sinking vessel. In the course of an hour, or rather less, the longboat of the *Scotia,* filled with men, was on her lee quarter. By the admirable arrangements, which were then made by Captain Collins for rescuing them, the men were taken on board without the least accident. This boat brought eighteen; the captain and five men had still remained on board, and were preparing to put off in the jolly boat. No little anxiety was felt for the safety of this little boat; in the course of half an hour, however, she was seen, and with two oars only she gained the *Roscius;* and the captain and his five men were soon taken on board.

To the credit of the poor master of the *Scotia,* be it observed, that he, Captain Jeans, was the last man to leave the sinking ship. The anxiety expressed by the men, who came in the first boat, for the safety of their captain, and, indeed, the terms in which the whole of his people, then and subsequently, spoke of Captain Jeans, showed how highly he was respected and esteemed by his crew; and if he had not been so, he would probably not have kept his ship afloat as long as he had done. Nor was the anxiety of Captain Jeans, for the safety of his crew, less manifest. The first question he asked, on coming on board the *Roscius,* was "Are all my people safe?" The captain and crew were all Scotch, and their conduct throughout reflected no discredit on their country.

When they came on board, they were worn out with continual exertion. The men had been night and day at the pumps, since the previous Tuesday; but, exhausted as they were, they immediately turned to, and with one accord went on deck and did duty with our crew; and no sooner were the boats cast adrift, than there was ample occasion for their services. A violent gale from the north-east set in, which must have rendered it utterly impossible for the people to have taken to their boats, and the violence of which, on the following day, must have been inevitably fatal, for it would have been impossible to have kept the pump going; and the sea already, even before the gale from the north-east set in, was making a clear breach over her, and threatening to carry away her poop-cabin, the last place of refuge left the poor people of the *Scotia,* except the top, where they had already stowed water and provisions, in the momentary expectation of being compelled to abandon the deck; and thus, providentially, were twenty-four human beings preserved from a watery grave.

The following is a letter from Captain John Jeans of the ill-fated *Scotia,* written to Captain Collins after Jeans had arrived in England:

Liverpool, England

Sir:—On behalf of myself and crew, I beg leave to express to you the heart-felt gratitude we feel for the assistance you rendered to us when, on the 5th inst., the vessel I commanded, the *Scotia,* bound from Quebec to Greenock, being water-logged, and myself and my people worn out with continual exertion,—and still, unfortunately, unable to keep her free, —you promptly consented to take us on, and thereby rescued us from certain death. For all the kindness and generous treatment we have subsequently received from you, we thank you from our hearts, and in the prayers of ourselves and families you never can be forgotten.

I am, sir, most gratefully yours,

JOHN JEANS.

To Captain John Collins, Packet Ship *Roscius,* N. Y.

Another original document is copied in this chapter. It was written by the passengers of the *Roscius* to Captain Collins:

On Board of the Ship *Roscius*
(Off Liverpool, December, 1839)

Dear Sir:—We, the undersigned, passengers of the ship *Roscius,* on the voyage from New York to Liverpool, deeply impressed with the admirable conduct you displayed on the recent occasion of your falling in with the wreck of the British ship *Scotia,* on the afternoon of the 5th December, and taking off the master and twenty-four men, found on that unfortunate vessel, cannot part with you without expressing to you our high sense of that energy of character and active benevolence, which actuated your character on that occasion, and happily made you, under God, the instrument of saving these poor men from the jaws of death. We feel that there were circumstances to be taken into consideration, connected with that event, which gave additional merit to the transaction—circumstances which required a great sacrifice of time and of interest, imposing a heavy expense on yourself, and were not unattended with risk to your vessel, perhaps the finest that ever sailed from New York, before the resolution of staying by the sinking ship, till such time as it was practicable to take off the people, cannot be fully appreciated or sufficiently commended.

Three days after the rescue Dr. Madden wrote a poem concerning the incident, which he dedicated to Captain Collins. Excerpts from the poem follow:

To Captain Collins of the "Roscius"
(On the Occasion of his falling in with the Wreck of the British Ship "Scotia," on the Evening of the 5th of December, and taking off the Twenty-four Men found on Board of that sinking vessel.)

Heroes can boast "their thousands, and their tens
   Of thousands," slaughtered on the field of strife—
And this was glory! O, what countless pens
   And tongues extol the waste of human life!—

*   *   *

Fame! let thy trumpet sound the warrior's praise!
   Glory be his who courts the world's applause!
Honor for him who seeks the public gaze,
   And acts for it till some new claim withdraws
   Its future smile. Thou, in a bolder cause,
And for a better need than human fame
   Didst rescue numbers from the very jaws

Of death itself, nor cared from whence they came.
To save and succor all, was thy sole end and aim.

O, when thou has to meet thy God on high,
   On record, then, that thrilling cry of theirs,
Which rent the air, on hearing thy reply,
   And made the wreck resound with thankful prayers,—
May this deed prove the death of all thy fears,
The life of all thy hopes! O, may it plead
   In thy behalf with Him, who ever hears
The poor man's prayer; and find thou has, indeed,
To his poor suffering members been a friend in need.

R. R. MADDEN

Ship *Roscius,* December 8, 1839.

CHAPTER FIFTEEN

Arctic Adventure

One of the great mysteries of all time is what happened to the expedition of Sir John Franklin, the Arctic explorer, whose ambition it was to discover the Northwest Passage from Europe to Asia.

Franklin sailed from England in 1845 aboard the *Terror* in company with the *Erebus,* which had his second in command, Francis Crozier, as master. Franklin had 129 personally selected men for the crews, and they were the pick of all England.

The last time the two ships were seen was off the western coast of Greenland when they were about to enter the Lancaster Sound area. After this, no further news came, and it was many years before even an inkling appeared of what might have happened to Sir John.

The two ships had gone southwest during the summer of 1846 and were caught in an ice pack the following winter.

There was no ice breakup the next summer of 1847, which saw the death of Franklin by heart failure on June 11.

Scurvy took the lives of twenty-four men by spring of 1848 when the ships were abandoned. The survivors started south on April 25 of that year but soon ran out of food. Then they were faced with the terrible necessity of eating their dead companions as they passed away.

Details will always be shrouded in mystery, but facts brought back by survivors of other expeditions supplied enough evidence of the barest outline of what really must have occurred during the weary, terrifying months and years when the largest and most publicized expedition of the nineteenth century was slowly wiped out by death.

The British government, after waiting what was considered a reasonable time for reports from Franklin, sent several craft out to search for the Arctic explorers. Among the ships dispatched were the H.M.S. *Investigator* and the H.M.S. *Enterprise,* which sailed in 1850. The vessels separated and lost all contact with each other.

It was not until many years later that the mystery of what happened to the *Investigator* was solved, and the survivors were able to tell their remarkable experiences in attempting to find the Franklin expedition. Their voyage had taken five years, and no other group had ever spent such a long, unbroken period in the Far North. When the survivors of the *Investigator* expedition returned, they were acclaimed by a House of Commons committee as having performed heroic deeds which rivaled the most valorous acts of warfare.

One of the *Investigator*'s crew, Henry Stone, told of his experiences. He described how at the start of the journey his ship sailed slowly down the Thames on her way from Woolwick to the sea in company with the *Enterprise,* both small ships, each less than 400 tons. I now quote excerpts from Henry Stone's written notes describing what happened after the two vessels separated:

Those were hard rough days. We were badly knocked about, but the captain—the famous explorer McClure [Sir Robert McClure and his crew were awarded 10,000 pounds for their Northwest Passage discovery]—simply said, "I shall expect to see all a-taunto men, before we pipe to supper."

It was a big order; but we worked like fiends, and carried it out—and the captain was so mightily pleased that he ordered us to splice the main-brace [a nautical term for "have a drink"], which we did as heartily as we had put the ship to rights.

We met a little ship called the *Plover,* which had been looking for the Franklin Expedition for two years and had neither seen nor heard of it.

We got round a place called Point Barrow, and then our ship was in a sea on which, I believe, no vessel had ever sailed before. We were, of course, a searching and not yet exploring party, and had to keep close to the land. We had a hard job when we were in the pack-ice—that is, a big space of floating pieces of ice which are more or less driven together—to keep the land in sight, and more than once we got aground.

At one time, when we were hard on a sandbank, we had to lower the boats and pull the ship off. We had been forced to provision the boats, in case the ship was lost, and one of them capsized, and we lost eleven barrels of beef, about 3,000 lbs. in weight. It was a splendid feast for the wild beasts—and how often we longed for it later when we were starving, and even mice became luxuries!

One of the first things we did in the Arctic was to fall in with some Eskimos who looked upon our ship with a sort of worship. They had never seen anything like her and thought she was a floating island. We had an interpreter, a Moravian missionary, who dressed like them, and spoke their language. When we first met the Eskimos we thought we should have to fight for it. They got their bows and arrows ready, and tore about with spears and knives, their hair streaming in the wind, which gave them a most ferocious look. We loaded our muskets and prepared for an attack; but the interpreter pacified them and there was plenty of rubbing of noses— which some of us thought was worse than battle—and bartering of mirrors, beads, knives, pins and needles for skins and weapons. It was hard to tell the women from the men. Neither sex was handsome and they don't wash much in the Arctic. A good coat of dirt is equal to an extra fur. . . .

Nothing could have been more terrifying than our position when the enormous icefields got us in their grip. We were like a boy in the hands of a giant. The ship was lifted up and crunched and nipped in the most amazing fashion. More than once it seemed as if the huge bergs, as they melted and fell with thunderous crashes, would smash us into fragments.

Day and night there was such a deafening grinding that you could not hear a man speak unless he put his mouth to your ear and howled into it. From that incessant din we changed, when we were frozen up, to a silence which was even more awful, and broken only by the howling of the wolves. The sun disappeared, and was not seen again for more than 80 days.

We spent our time in reading, telling tales, knitting, sewing, playing games, eating, drinking and sleeping. The best of all times was when we slept, I think, because then we could forget. There was no money on board, so we invented a currency of our own. Gun-wads were marked with an officer's initials, and he paid for an executed order with them instead of coins. On our return home these gun-wads were honoured just as banknotes would have been.

From first to last of our long Arctic imprisonment hunting was the chief joy and help. If it had not been for what fell to our bullets, we should have perished. The hunting gave us most of our excitement, too, and there were many narrow escapes from death, owing to frost-bite and wounded animals.

One day the sergeant of marines was out shooting musk ox. He had already tackled two, and had fired five bullets, killing one of the animals with the last. The surviving animal was charging him, and it looked as if the sergeant would be killed or have to run for it. But he stood his ground. Reloading his musket, he fired the screw of his ramrod; but even this did not stop the rush of the big musk ox. Then, as a forlorn hope, the sergeant fired the ramrod itself, and the ox fell dead almost at his feet.

We hunted anything and ate anything we could kill. Seals, foxes, deer, hares, wild birds, a small lot of fish, walrus— these were thankfully added to our lessening stores as the dreary weeks and months went by. Even a bit of wolf did not come amiss, and field-mice were real delicacies—when we got them. These little animals were about four inches long, and were found in great numbers when the thaw came.

The howling of the wolves round the ship was maddening and depressing, and they were so cunning that they could always slink away before we could shoot them.

Every incident at a time like that looms large in one's life, and I well remember the tremendous excitement there was one day when a polar bear hove in sight.

The bear came on towards the ship, but we were ready for him. We had pretty nearly finished the skinning, and our carpenter's mate was standing across him, cutting him, when an extraordinary thing happened. One of the bear's hind paws rose, and seemed to be going for the back of the carpenter's mate. The paw actually struck him. For a moment we had a bad scare; then we laughed, because we knew that some sort of nerve had been severed, and had made the bear give that queer slap with his huge paw.

That particular performance we understood on the spot; but we were thrown into further wild excitement by a strange discovery we made when we opened the bear. In his stomach we found all sorts of oddments, such as raisins, bits of pork, and even scraps of sticking-plaster. Instantly we supposed that there must be another ship, or at least a camp, not far away from us, and that somehow Bruin had got a meal out of them. How else could he have come by that strange mixture? Neither raisins nor pork could get to the Arctic without somebody taking them, and certainly sticking-plaster never grew in the ice.

A party was organized at once to go and search for the ship which might have been quite near. The party had already gone when the mystery of Bruin's meal was explained in a very simple, disappointing fashion. It had come from the *Investigator!* The captain's steward had thrown a tinful of refuse over the side, and the bear had sneaked up and done himself very well.

Even if there had been a ship near, I do not think she would have been found. During our second winter—1851–2—only three vessels out of thirteen, which had been searching for Franklin, remained in the Arctic—our own two and the *Prince Albert,* and not one of them was aware of the presence of the others! For a long time the *Resolute* and the *Investigator* were separated only by a few miles, yet none of us was aware of it!

Soon after we were in our winter quarters Captain McClure and a small party left the ship on a seldge, and got away to the North to a high point some 600 feet above sea-level, from which they had a vast view of the surrounding country. Then it was that, looking towards the spot where the land was supposed to exist, they discovered, to their amazement, that no land was visible, but that there was a Northwest Passage, a communication between the Atlantic and the Pacific.

The captain began to hurry back to the ship to bring the tidings, but he was overtaken by a snowstorm, and had to wander about all night. He might easily have perished, but he lived to get on board again, and to see that his discovery was duly celebrated. He had missed the ship by as much as four miles, and that is a question of life and death in a region where there is nothing to guide you and not a soul to help you.

For 300 years expedition after expedition had gone forth to find a Northwest Passage. Franklin himself had perished in the task—though he had found it; yet we in the *Investigator,* almost by chance it seemed, in searching for Franklin and his party, had discovered the long-sought-for open sea between the Pacific and the Atlantic. We had made the greatest maritime discovery of the age. We were the first and only people who had up to that time gone from the Pacific to the Atlantic by way of the North of America.

That wonderful achievement cheered us and filled us with pride for a long time; but of the Franklin Expedition we found never a trace. The ice had got us and held us, and the time came when our only object was to get away from the Arctic and save our own lives. Three unspeakably long years had passed—and we were just where we were to begin with. Starvation and death threatened us.

We suffered terribly from hunger, and, try as we would, we could not resist the temptation to get through our rations all at once. Our food for the day was issued on the previous evening, and often enough a man would take his allowance and get through it straight away. Next day he had to manage as best he could.

With provisions running short, and the long imprisonment and monotony telling on the men, that most dreaded of all diseases—scurvy—began to wreak havoc among us. Strong men became helpless, and loathsome to look upon and live with.

The captain determined to leave thirty men in the *Investigator,* and send the rest of us in two divisions—one to Beechey Island, where a relief ship, the *North Star,* was stationed, and the other to Mackenzie River.

We were in a state of deep dejection. Death had come amongst us, for a man had been claimed by scurvy and general debility. His hammock formed his shroud, and a shallow hole in the ice-bound earth was being dug for him. The gravediggers were at work, and the men who were to abandon the ship on deck ready to start off into the unknown.

Suddenly, coming, as it seemed, from the land of nowhere, we saw a man approaching. We could not believe our eyes or our senses. The man came on; then we saw that there were other men and a sledge and some dogs.

All who could stand or crawl crowded on deck; even the sick struggled out of their hammocks to join in the welcome to the men, to help raise a shout of joy, for it was found that these unlooked-for fellow-creatures were Lieutenant Pim and companions from the *Resolute,* and that the *Resolute* was at Dealy Island, not far away, and that Captain Kellett was with her. Lieutenant Pim had travelled for a month over the ice before reaching us.

Can you imagine what the meeting meant to men who had been three winters in the Arctic regions, who had made friends with starvation, misery, and gloom, and who were abandoning their ship as the only hope of salvation, and going from what was bad, certainly, to what might be infinitely worse?

We had come to search for Franklin, and in three years we had not seen so much as a sign of him and his party. They seemed to have vanished. Might we not also disappear?

Even the sorrow of coming burial was forgotten in the joy of this unexpected meeting. Hope sprang up, and we felt that we should really get away from a country the sight of which was gloomy and depressing.

Our captain went to the *Resolute;* the doctors of the two ships made a survey of the *Investigator's* people and declared that we were not fit to stay in the Polar regions any longer. We were ordered to go home—and never did men obey instructions more gladly than we did when we were told finally to clear out of the ship.

On June 3 we left our old ship to join the *Resolute,* and after a fortnight's incessant toiling over the ice with our boats and sledges we reached her. The Polar Seas gave us a final touch of their discomfort. All the journey was through slushy snow and melting ice. We were drenched and shivering, no hot food or drink was to be had, and the only way to keep liquids thawed was to put them inside the blanket bags in which we slept.

Again we had a bitter disappointment to endure. Did the Arctic mean to let us go? Certainly not. Perhaps it loved us too well; at any rate, it kept us prisoners for another winter, and claimed two more of our company, one of the mates dying on board the *Resolute,* and a man being taken a few days later when we had abandoned the *Resolute* and the *Intrepid* and gone to the *North Star.* The man who died in the *North Star* was very bad when we left the *Resolute,* and the doctors rigged up a dog sledge for him. On this he was dragged wearily over the ice, but he lived only four or five days after he got on board the *North Star.*

We returned to England, after spending nearly five years away, most of the time in the ice and darkness of the Arctic region.

The first signs of Sir John Franklin were ultimately discovered in 1859, when Captain Francis McClintock came across indisputable relics of the expedition.

CHAPTER SIXTEEN

The *Monitor*

⚓

Because of a flight I made in 1949 between Beaufort, North Carolina, and Cape Hatteras Light, when I was gathering material for a book, I became intensely interested in the story of the Northern ironclad, the *Monitor,* which fought a memorable engagement with the *Merrimac* in 1862. On the day of the flight we flew over the wreck and photographed the area.

The story of the battleship *Monitor,* often referred to as the "cheese box on a raft," begins with the outbreak of the Civil War.

The famous marine inventor, Captain John Ericsson of New York, offered his plans for the *Monitor* to the War Department early in the Civil War, but the government was only willing to accept the battleship if Ericsson put up the money for her himself. The Navy promised to pay the cost of the *Monitor* only if she won a victory in battle! Nevertheless, Ericsson was able to secure the financial support of three other men, John F. Winslow, John A. Griswold and Cornelius Bushnell.

Ericsson was not one to delay. He laid out the keel of what was to be the *Monitor* at Greenpoint, Brooklyn, and worked a veritable army of men in three shifts, around the clock.

Meanwhile, news that a Southern ironclad was under construction reached the North. Plans were rapidly pushed ahead, and Ericsson took over the work personally for the building of a warship.

The Southern ironclad was actually a captured Northern ship. On July 11, 1854, the keel of the first steam frigate in the United States Navy had been laid at the Navy Yard in Charlestown, Massachusetts. This proud craft was christened *Merrimac*. At the outbreak of the Civil War she was at the Norfolk Navy Yard, trapped there. The Northern officers set her afire to prevent her being used by the South.

The South needed battleships so desperately, however, that she was rushed into dry dock and repaired. Plans were outlined to make the *Merrimac* into an ironclad warship to fight the North. When she was finished, the *Merrimac* was renamed the *Virginia*, and made a trial run on March 6, 1862. Her original name has clung to her, however, and she is still recalled today as the *Merrimac*.

Back in Brooklyn, New York, the *Monitor* was launched on January 30, 1862. The ironclad emerged with a smooth, rounded inner hull, 124 feet in length and 34 feet in the beam. The outer hull was 172 feet long, and had a beam of 41 feet underwater. The vessel drew less than eleven feet.

Although armed with only two guns, the *Monitor*'s weapons were powerful eleven-inch smoothbores. Her smokestacks were designed so that they could be dismantled in action. Fifty-five feet forward of the turret, a structure which resembled a cheese box, was a pilothouse constructed of heavy iron legs. Here the captain was to command the ironclad during battle. The pilothouse was almost entirely hidden behind the visible part of the ship and rose less than four feet above the deck.

The turret was not the invention of Ericsson alone. In 1843 Theodore R. Timby had patented a revolving turret, and Ericsson agreed that Timby should receive $5,000 on every turreted vessel built. As constructed on the *Monitor,* the turret was a cylindrical iron tower covered with plates eight inches thick, twenty feet in diameter and nine feet high, placed in the exact center of the ship. Its revolving nature made it especially suitable for navigation in shallow southern waters. The guns could be loaded when turned away from the enemy and then brought back around and fired.

Ericsson announced that the ironclad was a "monitor to serve notice on England that all her wooden warships were useless," and his request that it be called the *Monitor* was granted.

John Lorimer Worden was chosen to command the new ship. At the outbreak of hostilities he had gone South with secret orders, and while trying to return was caught and imprisoned. Released in an exchange of officers, he had hardly recovered from this ordeal when he was commanded to report as captain of the *Monitor.* Commander Worden quickly won the respect and admiration of every man who served under him.

The Southern spy system, always more efficient than that of the North, soon reported that the Northern ironclad was nearly finished. As a result, extra construction crews were put aboard the *Merrimac.* A trial run was attempted on March 6, 1862, but because of the pilot's objections, the actual proving was delayed for two days. Even then, the guns had not been thoroughly tested; the officers and crew had been up all night; and the sailors were not as yet familiar with their ship. If all went well, however, Captain Franklin

Buchanan planned to utilize the trial run for an actual attack on the enemy.

At eleven o'clock on the morning of March 8, the *Merrimac* steamed down the Elizabeth River, accompanied by two wooden warships, the *Raleigh* and the *Beaufort*. It was an ideal day for the *Merrimac*, for there was no wind, and the waters of Hampton Roads were calm. Overhead the sun shone down out of a cloudless sky. Several miles away the Union Navy was enjoying washday, and a profusion of clothing hung in the sun on the decks of the *Congress* and *Cumberland*. Also at anchor in the Roads were the steamer *Minnesota*, the disabled steamer *Roanoke* and the sailing vessel *Saint Lawrence*.

Shortly after one o'clock in the afternoon, the Federal lookouts observed a strange-looking craft far up the Elizabeth River maneuvering slowly in the direction of the Union fleet. One officer aboard the *Congress* fixed his spyglass on the object and announced that not only was it the *Merrimac* approaching but she was coming out to do battle.

The struggle which followed proved a swift, decisive victory for the *Merrimac*, as neither the *Cumberland* nor the *Congress* could stand up against her, and the battle ended with the *Cumberland* sinking and the *Congress* surrendering. The victory was unquestioned and overwhelming. The Confederate loss in killed and wounded was 21, while there were 140 lost aboard the *Cumberland* and 136 on the *Congress*.

The *Merrimac* returned in triumph to Norfolk and there received hasty repairs before returning to finish her victory over the Northern Navy in the morning.

Meanwhile, in the North, the *Monitor* had made a trial run in a blinding snowstorm on February 27. Changes in the steering apparatus and adjustments in the engine proved necessary. By March 3 she was ready to be tested again. This time the trial was successful, and the vessel was prepared for the long trip to Hampton Roads.

At eleven o'clock on the morning of March 6, the *Monitor* sailed from Brooklyn in the company of the tug *Seth Low* and the steamers *Currituck* and *Sachem*. It was favorable weather when the journey southward began, and the *Monitor* made good progress until shortly after midnight on the morning of March 7, when the ocean became rough. By one o'clock in the afternoon a severe storm had developed, and the *Monitor* began to take in water through the hawsepipes and under the turret.

When the ventilator fans became wet and stopped operating, the engineers were overcome by smoke, and it was at six o'clock in the morning of March 8 that Captain Worden ordered a distress signal displayed. Shortly afterward the gale moderated, however, and the journey continued.

Then, around midnight, the storm increased, and the seas became dangerous again. Just when it seemed the *Monitor* could not survive any longer, the gale subsided as suddenly as it had returned. Cape Henry Light was sighted at three in the afternoon, and the remainder of the voyage was completed in calm weather.

A short time later, Captain Worden and his men were amazed to see great clouds of smoke rising from the direction of Hampton Roads, and they soon heard the noise of battle coming to them from over the water. Although his crew of fifty-eight were tired from the long, dangerous voyage from Brooklyn, Captain Worden ordered the decks made ready for action and the speed of the ship increased.

At seven o'clock that March night Pilot S. P. Howard was put aboard the *Monitor* to take her into Hampton Roads. He told the officers on the ironclad of the overwhelming disaster which had befallen the Northern Navy.

Just about the time that the *Merrimac* was returning to

her anchorage at Craney Island in the Elizabeth River, the *Monitor* sailed into Hampton Roads. That evening Worden wrote his wife that he had anchored the *Monitor* near the *Minnesota*. "The *Merrimac* has caused sad work amongst our vessels," his letter says. "She can never hurt us."

The *Merrimac*'s Captain Buchanan had been injured and was taken ashore the next day. The new commander was Lieutenant Thomas ap Catesby Jones.* He ordered the *Merrimac* to sail for Hampton Roads again at six o'clock that morning, in company with two wooden warships, the *Patrick Henry* and the *Jamestown*. Captain Thomas ap Catesby Jones had his first view of the new *Monitor* a short time later when he was summoned up on the deck by Lieutenant Davidson.

"What are you going to do about her?" asked Davidson.

"Fight her, of course," came the quick answer. "But don't forget that she has many advantages over us. Our knuckle † is our greatest weakness. If she concentrates her fire on that, she will make short work of us." The *Merrimac,* indeed, was vulnerable. Added to her many other faults, her engines were causing much trouble, and at times the great ship barely moved through the water.

After reaching the vicinity of the *Minnesota* the *Merrimac* opened fire. This was the signal for Captain Worden to steam his little ironclad directly for the huge three-hundred-foot enemy. The other Southern ships retired at once, and the *Monitor* and *Merrimac* began their epic encounter.

Captain Worden was naturally apprehensive about the ability of his narrow iron turret to withstand the direct fire of the *Merrimac*. His tiny *Monitor* with her two guns had challenged the mighty ten-gun Southern Goliath, and he and his men wondered at the result. But charge after charge from

* The "ap" in Thomas ap Catesby Jones is not, as it appears, a typographical error. It is a Welsh prefix.
† The place where the two surfaces of the vessel met at the water line.

the giant guns of the *Merrimac* were unable to penetrate the thick iron plates of the *Monitor*. The hours passed, with neither side gaining an advantage. All this time just one shot from the *Monitor* directed at the water line of the larger vessel would have sent her to the bottom.

At the end of three hours, the *Monitor* ran out of ammunition and withdrew to reload her turret. The Southerners jubilantly believed that they had defeated the Northern ship, but the *Monitor* was back in action immediately after the necessary fifteen-minute loading pause. While she was reloading, the *Merrimac* had been firing at the *Minnesota*, but once again she attacked the *Monitor* as her worthy opponent.

At times the smoke of the guns completely enveloped the two combatants, and on several occasions Northern witnesses feared that when the smoke cleared they would find that the *Monitor* had been sunk. But each time she reappeared, and at last the Union forces along the banks began to take heart. The *Monitor*, they observed, could maneuver in and out because of her light construction, greater speed and shallow draft, while the ponderous, unwieldy *Merrimac*, drawing more than twenty-two feet, became grounded time and again.

Finally, Captain Jones decided that if the *Merrimac's* fire could not penetrate the tough outer sheathing of the *Monitor*, he would try to ram the little vessel. But the superior speed of the *Monitor* enabled Captain Worden to slip out of the way and fire a devastating charge at the *Merrimac* from close range. At this very moment the *Merrimac's* guns were turned against the tiny wheelhouse of the *Monitor*, and a short time later a blinding explosion of powder and iron filled the pilothouse and knocked Captain Worden unconscious. His face and eyes were filled with paint and slivers of iron; his face was blackened and torn. One eye was permanently blinded. As soon as he regained consciousness, the captain ordered young Lieutenant Greene to assume control of his ship.

"I kept the *Monitor* either moving around the circle or around the enemy," said Greene later. "We knew that she could not sink us, and I kept right on pounding her as long as she would stand it. Once we ran out of the circle to adjust a piece of machinery, and I learned that some of our friends feared that we were drawing out of the fight.

"The *Merrimac* took the opportunity to start for Norfolk. As soon as our machinery was adjusted we followed her and got close enough for a parting shot. But I was not familiar with the locality, and I did not wish to take any risk of losing our vessel, so I came back to the company of our friends. Except that we were, all of us, tired and hungry when we came back to the *Minnesota* at half past twelve P.M., the *Monitor* was just as well prepared to fight as she was at eight o'clock in the morning when she fired her first gun."

By the time she left the scene of battle, the *Merrimac* was leaking steadily. Neither her officers nor her crew wished to withdraw, but, in addition to the leak, her engines were giving trouble and her smokestacks had been riddled by the *Monitor*'s shells; the engineer, Ramsay, reported that he "could hardly keep up steam." Shortly afterward the carpenter and the chief engineer appeared on deck to notify Captain Jones that the *Merrimac* was taking in so much water that she would have to return to Norfolk at once. Captain Jones decided that he could make no further effort to continue the battle. He ordered a gunboat sent ahead to prepare the Norfolk Navy Yard for the immediate dry-docking of his now badly leaking craft.

On the *Monitor*, Captain Worden had been taken to his cabin. There the surgeon removed the splinters from his eyes and face and swabbed his blackened skin with oil. A short time later Captain H. A. Wise of the Ordnance Department went aboard and told Worden that he had fought the most glorious battle in naval history.

"Have I saved that fine ship, the *Minnesota?*" asked the injured commander.

"Yes, and whipped the *Merrimac* to boot!" came the inspiring answer.

"Then I don't care what happens to me," replied Worden. A short time later he was taken ashore. He was the only one aboard who had been seriously wounded. Actually, the pilothouse had not been badly damaged, and there were only twenty-one minor indentations of the turret and deck.

Thus ended the battle between the *Monitor* and the *Merrimac*. Neither side won the fight, and there was not a man killed on either ship. However, this drawn engagement which was fought that Sunday afternoon in March 1862 was actually a Northern victory, for the *Monitor* accomplished her objective, and the *Merrimac* did not. The *Monitor* stopped the *Merrimac* from further depredations against the Northern Navy as was intended, but the *Merrimac* failed in her objective of sinking the *Monitor*.

President Abraham Lincoln, who went aboard the *Monitor* on May 6, gave Captain Jeffers, who had relieved Captain Worden, his own personal instructions two days later. He told Jeffers to sail out the next morning against Sewall's Point, fire two shots and await the *Merrimac*. If the *Merrimac* appeared, Captain Jeffers was to maneuver the *Monitor* toward two nearby ocean liners which would attempt to ram and sink the Southern ironclad.

Promptly at ten on the morning of May 9 Jeffers steamed across Hampton Roads under direct orders from his President. He fired two shots and awaited the *Merrimac*. But the Southern ironclad did not appear, and the *Monitor* returned to her anchorage.

There was a very good reason why the *Merrimac* failed to

answer the challenge of the Union ironclad. Norfolk was being evacuated, and the captain of the *Merrimac* had to choose between blowing up his ship or attempting to run for Richmond. Finally it was decided that the heavy ironclad could never negotiate the shallow channels which led to Richmond, and the decision was made to blow her up.

At four o'clock in the morning of May 11 the *Merrimac* was set afire. The oil and turpentine on the deck blazed fiercely, and at four thirty a terrific explosion shook the vicinity. Immediately there was a great cloud of smoke in the air, a cloud which soon gave way to bright, sparkling flames. Parts of the ship were seen flying in all directions as the powder and ammunition continued to blow up. The short, glorious career of the *Merrimac,* built to wrest supremacy of the seas from the North, was over. But every Southerner will always remember this ironclad battleship with pride, for the *Merrimac* covered herself with glory in her brief dramatic career.

Two hours after the *Merrimac* had been destroyed, President Lincoln was told of the event. The same morning he went to Craney Island to visit the smoldering ruins before his return to Washington. The *Monitor* passed Craney Island at eight that same morning, and the crew saw many fragments of their late opponent floating in the water.

On December 29, 1862, the *Monitor* left Hampton Roads in tow of the *Rhode Island,* heading for Beaufort, North Carolina. Also in the expedition were the *Passaic* and the *State of Georgia.* The *Monitor's* new captain, Commander John P. Bankhead, was worried about the weather and the ability of his ship to make the sea voyage. However, the ocean was calm when the ironclad rounded Cape Henry. Now the long trip southward began in earnest.

The following day, as she neared Cape Hatteras, the *Monitor* was hit by a wind which came in fresh from the southeast. By nightfall a storm began which increased to a bad gale in a few hours. The *Monitor* began to wallow helplessly in the terrific seas, and around midnight Captain Bankhead ordered a red lantern, the signal of distress, hoisted to the masthead. Shortly afterward the violent pitching and rolling became so serious that he ordered the towing hawser cut and the anchor let go. But this didn't prevent tons of water from pouring aboard.

Coming about immediately, the *Rhode Island* sent three lifeboats across to the sinking ironclad. The first lifeboat stove in her side against the hull of the battleship, but several men were taken off. The other two lifeboats removed a majority of the crew. Finally all but sixteen men had left the *Monitor*.

One old quartermaster was seen carrying his clothes bag under his arm and was reprimanded for trying to save his own belongings in an emergency. The quartermaster, without replying in his own defense, threw the bag into the lifeboat. Later, when the boat returned to the safety of the *Rhode Island*, the bundle was passed up over the side, and a tiny messenger boy was discovered inside, petrified with fear but otherwise unharmed. The quartermaster, realizing that the boy was too afraid to make the jump into a lifeboat, had jammed him into the bag and carried him off, thus saving his life.

When the three lifeboats and their occupants had reached the *Rhode Island* safely, another boat was dispatched to pick up the remaining sixteen men still aboard the doomed ship. Having to row into the wind, the rescuers made slow progress. Finally the light from the *Monitor* disappeared from view, and the men in the lifeboat knew that the proud Northern warship had gone down with all sixteen aboard, four officers and twelve men it was later discovered.

The lifeboat itself was in trouble and unable to return to the *Rhode Island*. When morning came an impromptu flag of distress was rigged—a large black silk handkerchief. A schooner hove in sight, and her captain noticed the black pennant. He fled the scene, evidently fearing an attack by pirates whose emblem was a black pennant. A few hours later, a second schooner sailed in close enough to recognize that the men were from the Northern Navy and took them aboard. They were later landed at Beaufort, North Carolina.

Both the *Merrimac* and the *Monitor* had short careers, but naval history was made that day in 1862. Although it was not the first engagement between ironclads, and although neither ship could have successfully sailed the open sea, it was only a question of time until better ironclads would be built which could steam across the ocean. The old sailing ships with their wooden hulls were no longer to participate in battle. The beautiful men-of-war with their splendid lines and billowing canvas sails gave way to the ironclads. Metal monsters had superseded the wooden sailing vessels in war as well as in peace.

Although it is not common knowledge, the general location of the wreck of the *Monitor* has been known for many years. At one time plans were made for salvaging her and towing her into Washington, D.C., to be placed on permanent exhibition. Unfortunately these plans were later abandoned.

It was my privilege in 1949 to fly out to sea from the coast of North Carolina near Cape Hatteras and inspect * the resting place of the Ericsson-built "cheese box on a raft," the ironclad which prevented Southern forces from gaining ascendancy over the Northern fleet eighty-seven years before. As we looked down through the clear water where the Northern battleship rested on the bottom, I wondered whether the government would ever raise the ironclad which saved the Union from defeat in 1862.

* I told the story in my *Strange Tales from Nova Scotia to Cape Hatteras*.

Others who have been interested in this wreck include Ben Dixon MacNeill and Raynor T. McMullen, whose ambition it has been to bring the *Monitor* up from the bottom and preserve her in a museum.

Early in the year 1955 I received a letter from a corporal named Robert Marx, then stationed with the 2nd Marines at Camp Lejeune, North Carolina, concerning the ancient ironclad. He had been scuba diving with a group of marines off the North Carolina shore, where hundreds of known wrecks are at the bottom of the sea, and became interested in an attempt to discover the *Monitor*'s final resting place.

Six years had gone by since my own flight, when at 300 feet flying away from the sun, we saw what was believed to be the turret and possibly the bow, before Robert Marx wrote to me, asking for assistance in finding the exact location of the *Monitor*. I couldn't really help him, for it had been only a brief look in unusually good weather when I had sighted the *Monitor*, if *Monitor* it was. Marx persisted in his efforts, however, and soon I learned that he had visited the underwater area where the *Monitor* lay on the bottom. In January 1955 he had made his first dive, but found nothing.

After exhausting research, Marx learned that the bodies of several of the *Monitor*'s crew had washed ashore at the time near the Civil War site of the Indiana encampment, not far from the present lighthouse. Later, he discovered Ben Dixon MacNeill, another *Monitor* enthusiast, and they pooled their resources. After making considerable progress, the two men finally dissolved partnership. Marx, however, continued to search.

On a perfect day, June 12, 1955, the *Monitor* and several other wrecks were seen by Marx and others from an airplane piloted by Corporal Holland. It was a day similar to that other perfect one six years before when Mrs. Snow and I had flown over the same spot in two different planes * to land at Cape Hatteras Light.

With the location carefully plotted, Marx finally arranged to visit the bottom in the area. On July 12, 1955, he achieved his objective when he descended in about forty-three feet of water to reach a troughlike area on the bottom, which he followed along until he came to a turret. It was the turret of the *Monitor,* which was showing four feet out of sand. He swam completely around the turret, examining the spacing of the large rivets. Then he swam to where he hoped the cannon ports might show and put his hands inside to feel hard-packed sand. There was no question, he had found the *Monitor!*

Since then several attempts have been made to rediscover the *Monitor,* all of which have ended in failure. This is easy to understand, for in a single storm the ocean bottom can be gutted out seven or eight feet, or sand can pile up an equal amount in the same period of time.

Possibly the *Monitor* should remain submerged in the sea bottom for all time, a fitting memorial for those sixteen heroes whose only grave will forever be the sea.

* In 1946 we conducted a similar diving operation with John Light over the hulk of the ancient pirate ship *Whidah,* which was wrecked at Cape Cod in 1717. We dropped a buoy in the sea, and later reached the wreck.

PART IV

WRECKS IN AFRICAN AND ASIAN WATERS

⚓

CHAPTER SEVENTEEN

The Castaways of the *Doddington*

On April 23, 1755, the East India Company ship *Doddington*, under command of Captain Sampson, left from England with four other East India vessels, and after an excellent run of seven weeks arrived off the Cape of Good Hope. She continued sailing on what her captain believed was a safe course until early on the morning of Thursday, July 17, when she struck a rocky shore some distance from the mainland about half an hour after midnight.

An account of the disaster which followed was left us by an officer aboard whose name has not come down to us. At the time of the crash, our narrator had rushed up on deck from below to find the seas rolling over the *Doddington* with great violence, each surge sweeping several victims into the ocean. After making his way to the port side, which lay highest out of water, he encountered Captain Sampson, who was completely overwhelmed by the disaster. The master told him in a broken voice that they were all going to die in the sea.

A few minutes later the *Doddington* snapped in two, and the captain was washed off and drowned. Our narrator managed to scramble back to the quarter-deck, although the small bone of his left arm was smashed.

In this awkward situation, he heard the cry of "Land!" A moment later, a sea hit him with such violence that he was knocked unconscious and did not awaken until daylight. Regaining his senses, he found himself transfixed to a plank by a large nail forced into his shoulder. In addition to the pain of his wound and his broken bone, he was so cold that he could scarcely move. Nevertheless, he realized that he probably owed his life to the nail the wave had pushed him against, for otherwise he would have been swept overboard.

Several of the more daring members of the crew had swum ashore to a small rocky island from the ledge where the *Doddington* had crashed. The lone survivor, he called out for help, but they were unable to assist him. Finally, mustering up his courage, he threw himself into the sea and battled the elements until he was safe ashore.

On landing, he found twenty-three other castaways, the only ones of the 220 aboard to save themselves!

The first thoughts of the castaways were to prepare some sort of shelter and to start a fire. Finding fragments of sail for a tent was not difficult, but building a fire was much more of a problem. When they tried to kindle two pieces of wood by rubbing them together, they failed miserably. Then they searched the rocks to find a substitute for flint and steel. After some time they found a box containing two gunflints and a broken file, but they still needed tinder. They finally discovered a cask of gunpowder which, to their great disappointment, proved to be wet. On closer inspection they found a small quantity still dry in the middle of the cask, and soon a fire was brightly burning.

After gathering the injured men around the fire, the able-bodied castaways went out in search of food and other necessities. A box of wax candles and a case of brandy were the first articles to be brought in. Another party returned stating that they had discovered a cask almost full of fresh water. This was of greater consequence than the spirits, as there was no fresh water to be found on the island. They had also seen at some distance several casks of water, flour and beer, but it was not possible to get down over the rocky cliff where the flotsam was.*

It now became necessary to provide some shelter for the approaching night. All hands began making a tent of the canvas that had been cast ashore, but the small amount of sail would not shelter the entire party. Even those who slept under the tent were exposed to the storm. Their frail dwelling was in danger of being blown away at any moment, but it did last the night. Before the next morning, however, their fire was scattered by the wind and extinguished by the rain. When daylight came and they renewed their search for useful articles from the wreck, they discovered that all the casks which they had seen the preceding night, except those filled with flour and beer, had been staved against the rocks. They secured those that were intact and then gave their attention to the extinguished fire, which they soon had blazing again.

It was then suggested that if they could find or make tools the carpenter might build a vessel to carry them to a port of safety. The carpenter agreed that with the help of everyone he might be able to build a craft.

Every survivor now talked of a boat. They were so excited about it that they could speak of nothing else. Not only did the men debate about how large she should be and how the craft should be rigged, but the optimistic castaways carried on

* Flotsam is cargo and other material washed overboard from a vessel.

long discussions as to what port they should steer for when she was finished.

That very afternoon some of them started looking for materials for the proposed vessel, but without success. On the following day they were luckier, finding four butts of water, one cask of flour, one hogshead of brandy and a small boat, which had been thrown up by the tide in a shattered condition. No tools were discovered except a scraper.

At daybreak the next morning one group had the good fortune to find a box containing files, gimlets, sail needles and an azimuth compass card. Other searchers brought back to camp two quadrants, a carpenter's adze, a chisel, three sword blades and, of all things, the ship's strongbox full of treasure! The bounty excited much interest, but thoughts of possible escape from the island overshadowed the finding of a treasure chest.

On Monday, July 20, 1755, they recovered more provisions, and also some timber planking, canvas and cordage. But they still had a long way to go, for the survivors needed many tools before the carpenter could start building the vessel in earnest. One of the Swedish seamen, Hendrick Scanty, who had originally been a blacksmith, found an old pair of bellows on the shore. He told his companions that if they could build a forge, he would be able to furnish the carpenter with nails and other necessary tools. Plenty of iron, he explained, could be obtained by burning it out of pieces from the wreck which had washed ashore.

Hendrick Scanty started to mend the bellows at once, and for the next three days all were busy. They put up a forge, and a tent shelter was erected over it. Then they collected lumber for the carpenter.

A few days later the carpenter announced that his plans were so far along that he would soon lay the keel for the craft, which, he decided, was to be a sloop thirty feet long and twelve feet wide. The smith's forge was now finished, and he and the carpenter began a workday system that allowed the sloop to be built rapidly and efficiently. Except during rainy spells, their labors continued day after day.

One afternoon there was a lucky find, when the ring and nut of the bower anchor were discovered. The blacksmith made an anvil from the iron, and after this he was able to supply chisels, axes, hammers and nails as required, and the carpenter and his helpers sped up the work from that time on. But there was still one great problem on the rocky, barren isle —food and water, which was already rationed far below the requirements for human existence.

As the sloop took form on the rocky shore, the castaways noticed smoke coming from far off on the mainland. Everyone started to talk about what the smoke might be. The carpenter decided to finish repairing the small boat so that a small number of the men could try to sail across and get help from whoever was responsible for the fire on the mainland. Seven weeks had gone by, their food and water was getting scarce, and they worried that they might eventually starve to death.

Three sailors were chosen for the trip and made arrangements for their voyage, stocking a scanty supply of food and water. The other castaways said farewell to them early one morning, and they rowed away from the island, setting their makeshift sail a short distance out. That night, soon after sunset, the survivors left on the island made a great fire on the highest part of the rocky ledge as a signal of hope for their friends.

Three days went by, and then at noon on the third day the men on the rock sighted the boat returning far in the distance. As it neared them they could see only one man rowing toward the rock and decided that the others had been lost.

In a short time a second man was sighted lying on the bottom of the boat.

Half an hour later the craft reached the rocky island. The two adventurers climbed out and knelt on the ground in thankfulness, praying aloud to the Almighty for having been saved. Exhausted, they lay down and could not rise for some time. When rested, the men told the other castaways the unhappy story of their experiences.

They explained how on the day of their departure, after sailing about six leagues * to the eastward, they reached a point just off a sandy beach, but there were great waves blocking their landing. With no alternative, they decided to row for shore, but soon a great billow caught them in its grasp. When the boat capsized, they were thrown into the sea and their companion was drowned. Managing to crawl ashore, more dead than alive, the survivors pulled themselves up above the reach of the tide. Then they began hunting for their boat. After some time, they found it a mile down the shore. They sighted a native, but he ran into the nearby woods.

Continuing their hike along the shore, they came across the body of their companion, which had been dragged some distance and evidently mangled by a wild beast. The sight of their dead comrade so disconcerted them that they resolved to attempt a return to their castaway friends at once.

Launching the boat, they started out through the surf, but a wave capsized them again. Struggling and swimming, they helped push the boat ashore, and pulled it up as far as they could above the reach of the relentless waves. Then they turned it upside down and crawled under, where they spent the night.

Awakening early the next morning, they discovered that

* A league is usually estimated to be three miles, although at one time it was 4.6 miles and at present in France is 2.49 miles.

several animals were prowling around. Some time later when a group of men came along, the two survivors crawled out to speak to them. The natives surrounded them and took the white men as prisoners.

Rifling the boat, the savages ripped off the sail and the lines, and then started to break up the hull itself. The two prisoners burst into tears, for this was more than they could endure. Begging the natives to stop, they finally won out in their entreaties, and the savages decided to let the men leave with the boat, which they planned to launch early the following morning.

The surf had gone down during the night, and the two sailors made a successful entry into the waves leaving the unfriendly but relenting natives behind them. All that morning the sailors rowed toward where they hoped the castaways' island was. Finally sighting the rocks, they landed successfully two hours later.

Their fellow survivors now realized that the news was far from encouraging. If they did run out of food, there was not much help ashore in the vicinity.

On Sunday, September 29, they recovered several casks of fresh water and more food, which had been washed ashore from the wreck by another extremely severe gale.

On October 11 the gannets which had flown away from the rock at the time of the shipwreck began to settle in great numbers and lay their eggs, and for nearly three months the castaways had a constant and plentiful supply of them.

All this time the carpenter was steadily working making the sloop's planking. Finally, in spite of his primitive tools, he announced to everyone's surprise, that the completion of the craft was in sight. On February 15, 1756, the survivors began loading supplies on their boat. They christened her *The Happy Deliverance* and then launched her into the sea.

Two days later, with everyone aboard, the sloop was sculled

and rowed out into deep water, where the sails were hoisted and a course set. There was great happiness as the craft began sailing away from the rocky island which had been the castaways' home for the better part of a year.

They hoped to reach the river St. Lucia, on the coast of Natal, but for twenty-five days contrary winds made their progress terribly slow. Rapid currents carried them far off their course, and they realized that soon they would have to change their plans and go ashore for water and food. A furious storm for the next three days prevented this, and the sloop shipped heavy seas from time to time. Each wave as it rolled over threatened to dash their craft to pieces. Then the seas went down, and soon a perfect calm developed, allowing them to cast anchor off a small native village.

A group went ashore in the boat, led by Arnold, a giant Negro crew member. With two seamen he rowed toward the beach where they landed safely. Arnold had brought along a string of beautiful amber beads as a present for the tribe, and for it received in return some corn, fruit, water in a calabash, and many promises for future food and drink if other exchanges could be made. Unfortunately, the wind began to come up, the sea roughened, and the boat was forced to return with only enough food and drink for about four days.

They continued to sail along the coast, the boat landing often to barter with the natives, who "everywhere thronged to the shore and received them with kindness." At length, on April 6, 1756, they arrived at St. Lucia, their destination.

Having landed there, they told the natives that they would like to trade with them, but the Indians said that they wanted nothing but small beads. On being shown some copper buttons, however, the Africans were satisfied. They brought fowl, potatoes, gourds and other provisions in exchange. No bullocks could be purchased, for the natives wanted to barter in copper rings large enough for collars. Finally they agreed to give five bullocks for a small piece of linen which caught their fancy.

The sailors remained at St. Lucia three weeks, traveling around the country and endeavoring to obtain such articles as they needed. The Indians set a great value on copper, and on being shown the handle of an old box, offered two bullocks for it, which was immediately accepted. The animals were quickly driven on board the vessel before the natives might change their minds.

On the eighteenth of May, 1756, the sloop weighed anchor at seven in the morning and set sail. Two days later the castaways arrived in Logoa Bay, where they found a trading vessel named the *Rose*, aboard which the survivors requested passage to Bombay. The treasure chest was now carefully transferred to the *Rose* under cover of darkness, and was not seen again for some time.

On the twenty-fifth of May the *Rose* sailed for Madagascar. One of the East India Company's ships, bound for Madras, was there, and the great treasure chest was transferred to it. In a month, treasure and castaways arrived safely home, and the unusual adventure came to an end.

CHAPTER EIGHTEEN

A Frenchman's Adventure in India

⚓

The English East Indian *Fattysalam* sailed on August 26, 1761, from Madras for Bengal. She was built at Bombay and had never been employed other than in the Indian Seas. When the ship left port she had more than five hundred people aboard, including French prisoners of war, and was towing a longboat loaded with pigs. The *Fattysalam* must have been in poor condition when she departed from Madras, for only two days later seven feet of water had entered the hold through her seams.

French Captain Kearney, who had been taken prisoner of war by the English at Pondicherry in January 1761, later wrote Count D'Estaing of his experiences aboard the ship,* and I refer to the letter from time to time.

On the same day that the water was reported in the hold,

---

* In the year 1778 Count D'Estaing brought his great French fleet into Boston Harbor. Hundreds of his men went ashore at Long Island.

Captain Kearney overheard two officers talking, one of them telling the other that the ship could not stay afloat more than two hours. The crew soon began throwing overboard everything that could lighten the vessel. At once Kearney went to a Major Gordon, who admitted that the ship might sink at any moment. Kearney then spoke directly to the captain of the *Fattysalam,* who was completely staggered by his misfortune.

"I would like permission to take the longboat, if you will permit it, sir."

"You'll only stay alive a few more hours. What difference will it make? It is not a practical solution of the problem where there are so many soldiers and sailors aboard."

Captain Kearney told the despairing master of the *Fattysalam* that he was going ahead with the plan to take over the longboat, throw the pigs overboard and get some of the passengers to safety.

"Please do not tell anyone about this," he concluded, "for if too many get in, the longboat will capsize. Why don't you join us?"

The captain, ignoring the tradition of the sea, agreed. Kearney and Major Gordon went aft to work out the details of the plan. They then proceeded to the cabin window, hauled in the cable on the longboat until it came alongside and began the transfer from the sinking ship. Although the vessel was a large one, she had no gallery, so that it was necessary for the men to let themselves down from the cabin window by rope directly into the boat. Captain Kearney ordered his servant, a husky man, to stand at the window with a sword and a hatchet and told him to kill anyone who tried to get into the craft unless he had been given permission.

One by one the Frenchman's chosen group lowered themselves down the rope and clambered across the pigs to occupy their assigned positions. Finally, with twenty-five people aboard, among whom were the captain of the ship and two young ladies, the cable was cut and they pushed off from the sinking *Fattysalam.*

Their first objective was to throw most of the pigs overboard, and the messy business was soon accomplished. Seven animals were kept so that the occupants of the boat would have a fair chance of getting to land without starving to death. They rowed out several hundreds yards from the *Fattysalam,* but people aboard the sinking craft then signaled that all was well and that the boat could be brought back to the ship. Of course, the signal was merely the desperate ruse of frantic men trying to save their own lives. If the boat had returned, scores would have jumped aboard, which would have capsized it at once, and no one would have been saved. They now rowed a greater distance from the sinking vessel, where Captain Kearney told his companions to take off their outer garments, for he had to make a sail.

Even the ladies were each obliged to give one of the petticoats they had on, which were only of muslin. All these things being joined and tied together, with our handkerchiefs torn into slips, formed a kind of sail, equally weak and awkward.

A short time later a fog rolled in, thick and impenetrable, and the East Indianman disappeared forever from view. She probably went to the bottom shortly afterward, with almost five hundred persons perishing when she sank!

Aboard the longboat Captain Kearney took stock of the situation.

We were in the open sea in a crazy boat which a single wave could have sent to the bottom, in the hand of Providence, without compass or any other rigging than our little sail which required all our attention.

We had not a drop of water, nor provisions of any kind.

We were constantly wet with the waves which entered our boat, and continually employed in bailing the water, with which we were incessantly inundated and, notwithstanding this fatiguing labor, we were shivering with cold, because we had very few clothes to cover ourselves, and those few were thoroughly soaked. In this state we floated at the mercy of the waves seven days and seven nights.

The only liquid to quench their thirst was a daily ration of a spoonful and a half of pig's blood. A pig a day was killed and everyone ate the raw flesh of the animals. By the seventh day there was nothing else to eat.

Then early in the morning of the eighth day, one of the group sighted land far in the distance. Surely enough, a speck was visible on the horizon. Despair turned to hope and the occupants of the crowded boat once more showed an interest in the future. Gradually the craft reached a point right off the unknown shore, but the booming of the breakers could be heard, warning the survivors that the surf was very strong.

A council of war was then held. The captain of the *Fattysalam* and many others who could swim voted in favor of steering the boat into the breakers and letting each person get ashore as best he could. Kearney objected, saying that the captain was condemning the two women and many others, including himself, to certain death.

"You'll not carry out your plan as long as I breathe," stated Kearney. "It is your duty to steer the boat until we reach a point where we can all get to land safely."

The Frenchman now drew his sword to show that he would enforce his demands and kill anyone who resisted him. An English officer named Scott then confronted Kearney.

"What? Does a single Frenchman, and a prisoner of war as well, here pretend to give law to us and dare to call us barbarians?"

"Sir," said Kearney calmly, "our common misfortune renders us all equal; I am free here as well as you, and repeat my pledge. The captain shall answer with his life for the lives of all our companions if he persists in his plans to land in the breakers!"

The captain suddenly gave in to Kearney, and ordered two Lascars, good swimmers, to stand beside the Frenchman and protect him. Taking the helm, the captain continued steering up the coast until he found a little inlet near a river's mouth which had relatively small waves. He managed the longboat so skillfully that the craft was guided toward a sandy beach where the left back of the river met the sea.

Just as the bow was striking the shore, twelve men, too impatient to await their turn, leaped out from the stern into deep water and were carried away by the force of the currents. Several minutes later all twelve had landed on the opposite bank of the river, after some narrow escapes from drowning. Those still in the boat waited for it to slide up on the left bank, where they stepped off onto dry land.

At a conference on the beach on the left bank it was decided that the most important need of the group was water. After a search a small lake was discovered. Every one ran to its banks and plunged into the water, where the entire party drank until they satisfied a thirst of eight days. Grass and shellfish were now eaten, and for two days the party did nothing but rest, eat and drink. The other group of twelve who had managed to get ashore were also busy finding food and drink.

With the two parties still separated by the river, it was agreed that each should hike up the bank in search of some settlement where they could join forces again. After walking an hour the thirteen met two fishermen who told them that they were in a country controlled by the Rajah of Asapour, which was a principality situated near the mouth of the Ganges. A quantity of rice and hog's lard was brought to the sufferers with the Rajah's compliments, and the next day they were taken to a small island where they were kept as prisoners. At this time they did not know the fate of the other twelve.

The group of thirteen remained on the island for seven weeks, their only food being black rice and salt fish. One of the women, Mrs. Taite, of Ireland, an expectant mother, had a good voice, and her singing to the natives was received with great pleasure. She thus helped to break down the barriers. Unfortunately, the water was so foul that thirteen of the twenty-five survivors in the two companies died, and even the twelve who survived soon had either fever or dropsy. Their complexion turned yellow, and they became so disfigured that no one, as Captain Kearney later wrote, "would have taken us for Europeans."

The two Lascar guards who had been assigned to the Europeans were told of their desire to escape and agreed to help them. Captain Kearney wrote a note to Barasole, where the English had a small factory, and the two Lascars set off with the message. It was a perilous journey, as they had to travel at night and there were four large rivers on the route. They finally reached Cattack, where they came before the local Rajah and told of the shipwreck and the Europeans' confinement by the Rajah of Asapour.

The Rajah of Cattack then had a message written giving an order for the prisoners to be freed, and the letter finally was brought back by the two Lascars. The island party started out with guides and met the survivors of the other group several hours later. By this time all the Europeans were walking skeletons, having lost much weight in the two months they had been prisoners.

The distance to Cattack required fourteen days of travel, and there were large rivers to cross. The two young Englishwomen, Mrs. Taite and Mrs. Nelson, soon became very ill from the journey. Mrs. Nelson died four days before reaching Cattack, but Mrs. Taite, whose baby was due in six months, arrived there safely. They were received with great kindness, and the food which they were given made a "delicious repast."

Journeying far ahead were the two Lascars, who finally reached Barasole, where they told the English of the survivors' terrible condition. The Lascars then were sent to Calcutta where they called on Mr. Vansittart, the English governor.

The governor lost no time in sending us relief; but on account of the distance, we did not receive it till twenty or twenty-five days after our arrival at Cattack. He used all his interest with the Mahrattas to obtain our liberty, but as they were not, at that time, on good terms with the Company, they refused to grant this favor to merchants. It was, therefore, necessary that Colonel Coote, the conqueror of India, should demand our release, which he obtained without difficulty.

The group now journeyed to Barasole, with Captain Kearney and his servant going ahead of the others in two dooleys * which he had hired for the trip. The journey to Barasole was almost fatal. Attacked twice by tigers, they lost one of the servants. One of the animals came back later and peered at the humans "with a most terrible look," but the men kept together and yelled, and the noise evidently made the beast go away without doing any more damage.

After reaching Barasole, Captain Kearney met some Englishmen who were sailing for Bengal, and the Frenchman's party joined them. Seven days later they reached Calcutta, where Kearney and his servant went aboard the *Plassy*, whose master was Captain Ward. While on board the *Plassy* he was

* A little chair or barrow, resembling a litter, carried by four men.

befriended by a Captain White of one of the East India Company's troops. Kearney explained that he was one of the survivors from the ship *Fattysalam* which was lost off the coast of Coromandel. On hearing this, Captain White went to his cabin and brought the surprised Frenchman a complete change of clothing from head to foot. Kearney, who for ten weeks had worn the same shirt, was overwhelmed. Captain White then offered Kearney some chocolate to drink, but it made Kearney so faint he could not touch it. He drank some tea, which was all he could swallow.

They journeyed up the Ganges River to Calcutta, but on the way his faithful servant was attacked by a violent fever and died in a Calcutta Hospital. Captain Kearney visited the governor at Calcutta, Mr. Vansittart, who assigned 120 rupees a month to him for living expenses. His benefactor, Captain White, lent Kearney 300 rupees, with which he bought linen and clothes.

It was not until two months later that Kearney was told to go aboard the *Hawk*, but as he then was ill from fever, the ship sailed without him. The Frenchman now attempted to get a loan from Governor Vansittart but failed.

On February 2 he left Calcutta and eventually embarked in the *Holdernesse* commanded by Captain Brooke. There he joined fourteen other French officers, all of whom were prisoners. Eventually he arrived in London and was permitted to go to his homeland a month later.

CHAPTER NINETEEN

The Whitmonday Wreck

⚓

Three of the many ways to entertain yourself at home in these times are reading books, watching television shows or listening to the radio. The story in this chapter is of such an unusual nature that probably if it was told to you as fiction in any of these media, you would find it unbelievable. But truth can be stranger than fiction.

Included in this tale are a shipwreck off the coast of Africa, a horse which rescued sixteen people, and a gallows erected on the way to the beach to hang people daring to visit the scene of the disaster against orders.

By the early 1770's the Dutch East India Company had developed a prosperous business in Africa and Asia and operated a great fleet of ships to carry merchandise and goods back and forth from Holland. Their vessels visited almost every important seaport, while their profits mounted rapidly.

It was inevitable that a ship should occasionally be wrecked and lost.

On the morning of Whitmonday, June 1, 1773, the ship *Jonge Thomas* of the East India Company anchored with three other company craft in the so-called East India Roadstead near the Cape of Good Hope. The local governor had declared that this roadstead was not to be used by company vessels as an anchorage.

Late that afternoon threatening clouds appeared over the horizon, and soon winds were sweeping in from the northwest. Within two hours the winds had reached high velocity, and shortly afterward "violent hurricanes and showers of rain" hit the roadstead.

The *Jonge Thomas,* anchored in a more exposed location than the other three ships, now took the full brunt of the storm. After twenty minutes she lost her right anchor. Another was hastily put over, but the cable snapped almost at once, leaving the left bower as the only hope. Ten minutes afterward the left bower cable snapped, and the *Jonge Thomas* was in serious trouble. Beginning to drift as she was battered by wave after wave, she was buffeted slowly up the coast in a northerly direction.

She approached the island of Paarden, also known as Horse Island, late the next afternoon. Shortly after midnight she was caught in a great billow and shattered apart on an underwater ledge, one hundred yards from the sandy beach beyond.

At daylight a citadel guard, sighting the wreck, dispatched a messenger to the governor of the province, who ordered a lieutenant and thirty men sent down to the scene of the disaster. A Dutchman named Woltemad, who had come to South Africa from Holland and was keeper of the local zoo, near the botanical gardens, had gone out to the fort near Paarden Island early that morning. Even before the governor learned of the shipwreck Woltemad had reached the citadel, to deliver a bottle of wine and a loaf of bread to his son, a corporal stationed there. When Woltemad arrived at the fort, he was told that his son had gone down to the shipwreck with the other soldiers.

The father galloped his horse over to the shore, where he was overwhelmed by the magnitude of the tragedy. Wreckage littered the beach, and bodies of victims were washing in everywhere. After giving his son the refreshments, Woltemad told the youth that he couldn't stay there on the beach without trying to save some of the people still alive on the wreck. He had often swum his horse out into the breakers and was confident that he could rescue at least a few of those still alive.

Galloping his mount into the surf, he soon reached the area of the wreck. The animal was guided out under the lee of the chains, where Woltemad ordered two of the sailors to clamber down and grab a line which he tossed up to them. With the two men clinging to the horse, it started swimming for the beach. Ten minutes later they were safely ashore.

Again and again Woltemad repeated his brave act until he had saved a total of sixteen people! By this time, the exhausted steed began to show signs of weakening, and the rider was also tiring fast.

Walking the animal up from the beach Woltemad tethered it in some nearby bushes. He then sat down on the grass to get his wind back, when suddenly a man came running to him.

"Please save my wife," he entreated, "for she is right by the ship's figurehead. I implore you, save her!"

Woltemad grumbled a bit and then stood up. Against his better judgment he went over to his horse, and in spite of a warning from his son, climbed back on the weary mount and guided it down to the beach. Soon they were approaching the wreck again. Reaching the bowsprit, he tossed a line to the woman and watched her as she grabbed it. Then he pulled her close to the horse. Suddenly several other survivors leaped into the sea around him. One man, frantic with fear, grabbed the horse's tail, another clutched the reins and still another his mane. Soon there were eight desperate people in the water, all attempting to hang onto the animal. A moment later, the steed gave up the unequal fight. It rolled head over heels and drowned, taking all eight persons with it to the bottom.

Back ashore, the governor had arrived and personally supervised the erection of a gibbet for the hanging of unauthorized visitors. After finishing the gallows, he had a huge warning sign posted which read as follows:

ALL PERSONS CAUGHT PASSING
THIS POINT WILL
BE HANGED
WITHOUT BENEFIT OF TRIAL OR
SENTENCE OF ANY SORT
BY ORDER OF THE GOVERNOR

All along the coast the residents heard of the shipwreck and started to visit the scene, where without question they could have saved many of those who drowned. In spite of their eagerness to help they were forced back by the lieutenant and his thirty soldiers, who threatened to hang them at once.

The residents gathered just outside of the restricted zone, close enough to witness many scenes of vicious brutality. While the soldiers were gathering spoils from the wreck, they ignored the shrieks and cries of the unfortunate people from the *Jonge Thomas*. In the freezing weather, many of the survivors died within a few hours on the beach, not understanding why they could not be cared for, since the soldiers were all around them gathering up the merchandise.

One unhappy survivor was the ship's gunner, who had stripped himself naked so that he could swim ashore more easily. He had lowered himself into the water with his sea chest of clothing, to which he clung. Near the shore a great wave separated him from the trunk, but another billow washed him up on the sand alive. Cold and shivering, he located his possessions on the beach, but now he ran into unexpected opposition. Just as he was about to open the sea chest to remove his clothing so that he could dress, a soldier threatened to shoot him for taking goods from the ship.

"It's my own sea chest, and here's my key to it still around my neck," he explained, but the soldier said that he had his orders and was carrying them out.

"Why, there's my name painted on the chest," the gunner explained. It did no good, for when he started to use the key the soldier struck him a blow with his bayonet, and the survivor gave up for the moment.

But the poor man was naked and freezing. Once more he appealed to the soldiers for mercy, asking for clothes from his own supplies, but they refused again and hit him several more blows.

The gunner retreated into the brush, and all that day suffered intensely from the piercing winds which hit his defenseless body. When the sun went down he came out on the beach again and made his final appeal to the soldiers. As he talked, however, he noticed that his chest had been broken open. He walked over to it. It was empty, for the looters had taken every last garment he owned!

He made his way to the nearby town, where his plight excited the pity of the town burgher. The kindly official took off his own greatcoat then and there and gave it to the gunner to wear. For the next few days, in nothing but the greatcoat, the wretched man wandered around town, begging for food and shelter. He was not alone, for more than a score of other unfortunate survivors from the shipwreck, also without food and shelter, were doing the same thing.

Finally a representative of the East India Company arrived on the scene and gave the sufferers funds, with which they bought clothing and food. The unlucky men were then lodged in the local inn until the arrival of a packet boat, on which they journeyed back to their native Holland.

Arriving in Holland, the survivors told of the heroism of the zookeeper Woltemad and of his rescue of sixteen people from the *Jonge Thomas* before his unfortunate death. The directors of the Netherlands East India Company were so impressed by this brave act that the next ship they launched was christened in his honor, *Woltemad*. A tablet was placed at the stern telling of his sacrifice at sea, while orders were sent to Africa to promote Corporal Woltemad and give him other honors.

Unfortunately, by the time the notice of promotion and honor for Corporal Woltemad reached the citadel the young man had left for Batavia. He had applied for the position of zookeeper which his father had enjoyed before his death, but was turned down in derision. Discouraged, he had asked for and obtained a discharge from the service, after which he sailed for Batavia. He died there a few weeks after his arrival, before he could learn of the tribute paid to his father and of his own forthcoming promotion.

CHAPTER TWENTY

The *Winterton's* Castaways

The story of the castaways from the *Winterton* has one of the strangest endings of any that I have written about shipwrecks.

In the spring of 1792, the ship *Winterton,* an East Indiaman, with 117 persons aboard, sailed out from England under the command of Captain Dundas. She arrived safely at the Cape of Good Hope, but shortly afterward her luck ran out. On leaving the Cape, Dundas had intended to follow what was known as the outside passage to India. When he encountered light, variable winds, however, he decided to abandon his original plans and bear away for Mozambique Channel.

In order to avoid a shoal which he knew to be incorrectly located on the admiralty charts, the captain steered east. When he estimated that he was far enough eastward of the shoal to avoid it, he altered his course in spite of the fact that it was night. Three hours after he changed direction, at about midnight, the ship struck heavily in the darkness. The boats were instantly put on the davits and lowered. When soundings were taken, they found deep water within fifty yards of the stern of the vessel.

Every trick known to men of the sea was tried to get the *Winterton* off the ledge, but without success. Daylight soon showed them that the ship had struck a reef about six miles from shore, whereas Captain Dundas had believed his position to be at least sixty miles from land.

As the tide ebbed, the ship strained violently, bilged and soon began to leak. The rudder then snapped off, and the copper sheathing of the vessel came up alongside her. Hopes were still high that they would succeed in getting her off during the next tide. Working hard to lighten her, the crew began to throw the guns overboard one by one, but only half the weapons had been dumped into the sea when a strong sea breeze set in. Nevertheless, they continued to jettison many other heavy articles. At high water they again tried all possible methods to get her off but failed. By this time the leak had gained on the pumps in spite of all their efforts.

The ship was now given up as hopelessly lost, and the safety of the passengers and crew was the next problem. The masts were cut away in order to lighten the strain on the vessel, and several spars were tied together to make a raft. The captain ordered every cask of liquor staved in so the crew would not drink to excess.

Toward evening, a party was ordered to go ashore in the yawl to prepare a landing place and set up camp. The craft left the ship and remained overnight. The wind soon increased, and three of the boats were dashed to pieces by the powerful surf. Throughout the long night the ship beat violently against the rocks.

When daylight set in, all hands began to construct rafts for the escape from the wreck, using such materials as they could find. Four rafts were finished, loaded with twenty persons each and pushed away. All reached land within a few hours. The breeze continued to freshen, and the hawser which held the ship's stern to the wind parted. She drove broadside on the rocks, and the sea soon made a complete breach over her. The hull started to break up, and every one left on the wreck crowded to the quarter-deck and poop, as they were the only places which offered any chance of safety. Shortly afterward the vessel went completely to pieces. Some of the fragments with their human cargoes were driven ashore, but the captain drowned in the sea.

For several days, portions of the wreck continued to come up on shore, often bringing with them some part of the crew. When the survivors were gathered together and a ship's company * check was taken, it was found that the captain, the first mate, three young ladies and forty-eight seamen had perished.

Hardly had the officers finished counting the survivors when the natives of the area discovered the wreck. Flocking to the scene, they seized everything of value that had either been saved or cast on shore, and threatened any person opposing them with instant death.

At length the survivors of the *Winterton* journeyed overland to reach Tulliar, the residence of the king of Bab, by whom they were kindly received. The yawl, which had been sent ashore the evening before the vessel broke up, was then dispatched to Mozambique to obtain a ship to come to their rescue. After sailing for some days, the craft reached the coast of Africa, but the crew decided the natives were unfriendly and steered for Sofala, a Portuguese settlement, where they arrived safely.

* Ship's company includes all persons aboard regardless of standing.

Unfortunately, only one vessel a year visited Sofala, and the last had sailed about a month before. As there was no immediate hope of relief for their companions here the crew set sail for Delagoa Bay. Contrary winds and the leaky state of their boat, however, soon forced them to return to Sofala. This time the governor received them with little ceremony, insisting on the whole party going to Senna, an inland settlement.

For five weeks they traveled through a hot, desolate country, menaced by the wild beasts with which the area abounds. The strain and the bodily tortures which they underwent on this journey were too much for several of the party, who died shortly after their arrival.

Many weeks of hardship followed. At length, five months after leaving Madagascar, two of the forty who started reached Mozambique. Here they hired a vessel and proceeded to the rescue of their unfortunate comrades. By the time they returned, however, they discovered that disease and despair had ended in death for nearly one-half of the survivors from the wreck. The others were put aboard, but seven of them died on the passage to Mozambique. Thirty more survivors, in spite of every attention lavished on them by the governor and inhabitants, died within two months of their arrival.

When the others were so far recovered as to be able to sail, they again hired a vessel to carry them to Madras, but the ship was captured by a French privateer. Part of the crew were taken on board the privateer, while the others were allowed to stay on the captured vessel,* with orders to proceed to Mauritius with all possible speed. The privateer then continued her cruise. In a few days she fell in with a Dutch East Indiaman and was captured. The survivors of the crew

* This group eventually reached England.

of the unfortunate *Winterton* were identified and then set at liberty. Finally they arrived in Madras, from which they sailed for England in the sloop-of-war *Scorpion*.

After all their hardships and struggles, these survivors of the *Winterton* never arrived in England. Nothing was ever heard of the *Scorpion* again, although the East India Company caused the most diligent search to be made for the missing warship. The ship had vanished from the face of the sea.

Thus did many of the survivors of the *Winterton* achieve freedom at first, only to lose it again. Their more fortunate companions, who had been released by the French privateer, eventually managed to return to England.

CHAPTER TWENTY-ONE

The *Fanny* in the Chinese Ocean

⚓

In the year 1803 there was a British marine officer named Page who was anxious to advance himself in the merchant service. Still, he did not wish to be tied down aboard any particular ship until he had had a chance to take a long trip, as he had been left a moderate sum of money by the death of a relative. Mr. Page decided to go on a voyage aboard the ship *Elphinstone* to India, where he would then seek a position on another craft.

Leaving England during the month of October, 1803, he reached Bombay the following July, where he visited various vessels then in port. He soon secured a berth as second mate aboard the *Fanny* which was about to sail for China. His commander was Captain Robertson, an even-dispositioned master. The first mate, however, was extremely excitable and not a good officer.

On August 8, 1804, the *Fanny* got under way. Her voyage

was without incident until three weeks later when she met with a strong gale, which in a short time grew to the dimensions of a real typhoon. It began to blow so hard that it was impossible to carry any sail. Then suddenly the wind went down, and a dead calm developed, as the eye of the storm passed overhead.*

Half an hour later the typhoon came back with renewed violence and was soon shrieking through the rigging of the *Fanny* worse than ever. So furious was the wind that it swept the top of each wave off, covering the ocean with thick foam so that it resembled a boiling cauldron.†

About nine o'clock the foremast went by the board, tearing away the rudder as it swept astern. When three feet of water was reported in the hold, all hands were ordered to take turns at manning the pumps. Driving to and fro, the ship was completely at the mercy of the wind and sea. The burden of these tribulations proved too much for the captain, who lost all initiative, and the mate, who went out of his mind.

Second Mate Page, realizing that no one really was in command of the *Fanny*, decided to offer his services in running the ship. He reported to Captain Robertson, who told him to manage the ship any way he liked.

"I have no desire to make further decisions on the *Fanny*," were the captain's final words.

Page at once went below where he encouraged the sailors to do their best at the pumps, staying with them until they more than held their own against the incoming water. Now the ocean began to build itself up so fearfully high that the waves could not be distinguished from the clouds. The fury of the sea continued until midnight, when the winds at last

* All hurricanes and typhoons are said to have an eye, or center, around which the storm rotates.

† The location of the *Fanny* when the gale hit was 17 degrees 42 minutes north latitude and 112 degrees 18 minutes east longitude.

seemed to have spent themselves. By constant pumping, the men won a great victory, reducing the water in the hold until it was only nine inches deep.

Nevertheless, without her rudder the *Fanny* still drifted at the mercy of the waves. The wind had diminished, but suddenly all aboard heard an ominous, cracking sound. It was the great mainmast, which came smashing down on deck, killing one man and injuring five others as it slid off into the sea.

After getting a jury-mast rig set and putting on a new rudder, the *Fanny* sailed toward the island of Hainan, located off the coast of southern China, across the Gulf of Tonkin from Indochina. There she anchored a quarter-mile from the beach.

The chief mate, although still mentally unsettled, took his servant and four men ashore in the longboat to get a supply of water. While the six were ashore, a wind began to blow, increasing by the minute. The anchor cable snapped, and the *Fanny* drifted out to sea. Several days later she beat her way back to the island where she again anchored off another section of Hainan.

By now provisions were getting scarce on board. Forbidden by their rulers to sell food to the white people, the natives did give the Europeans water. Finally there was nothing left to eat but four casks of dried peas, and all on board were reduced to half a pound of peas for their daily diet.

A message was sent out from Hainan that the chief mate and the five sailors had been taken prisoner. Marched across the country to the beach opposite where the *Fanny* lay, the six men were escorted down to the shore and abused in sight of their shipmates.

Mr. Page went ashore to bring back the prisoners, but the savages refused to deliver them without ransom. Mr. Page and Captain Robertson then decided to fire on the town and shell the natives into submission with the four mounted six-pounders. The *Fanny* came abreast of the settlement, and after capturing a native in a canoe for a hostage, the crew began making plans to bombard the inhabitants.

Suddenly the wind shifted, blowing with terrible intensity offshore. The mainsail split, the rudder broke away from the stern, and the ship began drifting before the wind. Soon far at sea, she encountered the Paracels, a group of islands then unexplored. The *Fanny*'s helpless course continued until the twenty-first of November when a second rudder was finished and hung.

That night they stood toward the southeast. At daylight, with dangerous rocks and sands in every direction, the anchor was let go. Their only hope was to repair the jolly boat and search for a passage through the reefs, nine of which could actually be counted from the masthead. Work on the craft took two days, during which time the ship was driven nearer the lee rocks, as the anchors did not hold.

When launched, the jolly boat leaked so much that she proved useless. When Captain Robertson saw that a reef was only a hundred yards distant from the ship, he ordered the anchor weighed and sail made to escape the danger. Before the command could be carried out, however, the wind suddenly shifted and drove the ship hard against the reef.

In this manner, at one o'clock on November 26, 1804, the *Fanny* smashed herself high on a ledge. The mizzenmast had to be cut away to prevent the ship from going to pieces. As it was high tide when the vessel struck, nothing could be seen except shallow water. Then, as the tide went out, the rocks began to show, and at low water great areas were dry for miles around.

Cast away on an unknown reef * at 9° 44′ north latitude

* Probably on or near what is now called Cuarteron Reef.

and 113° 51′ east longitude, the survivors took stock of the situation. Fifty-six persons were aboard a vessel which might go to pieces at any moment in the raging sea, with no possibility of rescue by others.

The castaways decided to cut off the poop or stern deck and build two flat-bottomed boats out of it. Aided by all the Lascars but one, who swore he would rather die than work, the two floats were rapidly completed.

Mr. Page, the captain and the gunner were the only Englishmen on board, and Page proposed that they and the captain's servant flee the ship in the jolly boat should the *Fanny* sink, to which the captain agreed. Meanwhile the water rose in the hold. On the twenty-ninth of November, there were two feet seven inches; on the morning of December 4, nearly ten feet, and at noon the vessel's hold was completely full.

As the days went by the sailors would often go out on the rocks at low water in search of shellfish. One afternoon they found a quantity of rock oysters, but the taste was so strong that few could stomach them. Sometimes two or three fish, left by the tide in holes of rocks, were caught.

Two weeks after the ship struck, the combination of salt water and cotton in the hold began to give out a terrible stench, with fumes so strong that they blackened a silver spoon between decks. Many of the survivors, including the captain, became violently ill from its effects. Their heads began to swell, and their faces soon assumed grotesque caricatures of their regular features. Often the victims were so terribly disfigured by morning that their companions failed to recognize them! Four men died in one week, and most of the others became ill. The sickness and death depressed the carpenters, and work on the rafts consequently slowed up.

On the twenty-second of December a brig was seen to the eastward, standing towards the wreck. Anxious to avoid any communication with pirates, those on the *Fanny* did not signal at first, but when the craft showed American colors, the castaways hoisted a British flag, union down to show they were in distress.

Two miles away the American brig *Pennsylvania* hove to and sent off her boat, but they could not find the passage through the reef. Mr. Page went out in the jolly boat with three men hoping to guide the rescuers to the *Fanny*. The Americans came abeams and waved for Mr. Page to come out through the surf, but the waves were too high for the jolly boat, and so they gave up.

Seeing that they could not get through the waves, the Americans returned to their ship, which made sail from off the reef. The jolly boat went back to the wreck with her desolate crew who believed the Americans had deserted them. The rescue vessel appeared again at noon when the wind had gone down, however, and sent off her boat which came through the reef without much trouble this time.

The Americans brought a note from their captain offering to remove the *Fanny*'s passengers and crew from the wreck. Captain Robertson refused, declaring that he would take his chance in the floats, though he announced that any of his people who wished to transfer might do so. The American chief mate took Mr. Page aside and told him that he was welcome to come on board the brig. Mr. Page decided not to go, as he was afraid that his conduct might be misconstrued. "I am sorry Captain Robertson has taken such a desperate resolution, but my duty is with him," were his words.

The chief mate of the *Pennsylvania* returned to his ship. When his captain learned that Captain Robertson and Mr. Page would not change their minds, he ordered his chief mate to return to the *Fanny* with sugar, vinegar, bread and other supplies. To lighten the floats he offered to take aboard four persons who must all be Christians, and four Portuguese were chosen to go. When this party reached the brig, she sailed away.

Because of the good solid food he had received, the captain soon regained his health. The floats were finished on the last day of the year, and indeed they were strange sights, resembling two gigantic boxes. The bows projected at an angle of forty-five degrees, with each float seventeen feet long at the bottom, and twenty feet long at the gunwale. They were five feet deep, with an extreme beam of eight feet.

On the fourth of January, 1805, the crew of the *Fanny* embarked in the floats, after having been nine weeks at the wreck on the rocks. The captain, Mr. Page and twenty-three other Europeans were in the first float, while twenty-four Asiatics were in the second. Malacca, 1,100 miles away, was the nearest place they dared to land. Hopeless as their plan seemed, the survivors of the *Fanny* resolved to attempt sailing that great distance. Eleven muskets with some ammunition had been taken from the ship onto the captain's float. Fastening the jolly boat astern, they started on the long journey.

Luck was not with them at first, for in attempting to get over the reef, both floats grounded, beating violently on the ledges for two hours. Finding a deep area in the midst of the reefs, they cast anchor for the night. When morning came with an extremely high tide, both floats were freed.

When the captain's float reached the open sea, the gunwale was only nine inches out of water, with the spray constantly washing in. Another plank, nine inches wide, was run along, and over it a length of canvas was secured. Although there was less spray, still it did not keep them dry. Finally two Lascars were placed in the small boat, lightening the float a trifle.

On the eighth of January, daylight brought no appearance

of the Lascars' float, and it was feared they had perished. The sea ran higher and higher; but the little craft astern rode the waves remarkably well. Toward midnight January 9, however, a heavy sea capsized the jolly boat. Both her crew were washed out and were heard exclaiming in despair, "Allah, Allah!" One seized the towrope and was taken into the float but the other drowned. The boat was then cut away.

By the seventeenth day of the voyage the seas became so tremendous that the situation was very grave. The captain had lost the use of his limbs, the dreaded scurvy had broken out among the members of the crew, and one man passed away in excruciating agony.

On the twenty-sixth they were driven westward by the current to Pulo Tingey, an uninhabited island. Here for two days they engaged in an unsuccessful search for some antidote against scurvy. Finally they filled their casks with fresh water and resumed their course.

A brig was seen at the entrance of the Straits of Malacca, bound to the Island of Bentang, for pepper. Her captain gave the Europeans some provisions. He told them to keep close in to the Malay shore, as the straits were infested with pirates. In a recent engagement with them, the chief mate of the brig had been killed and the captain himself had been wounded.

For five days the float crossed the straits to Malacca, which they reached on February 4, a month after their sailing. The float was safely moored, and the sick were removed to the local hospital.

Thousands now came to visit the adventurers after their sensational journey, and the men of the settlement helped them in every way they could. The captain was taken on shore and properly treated. Mr. Page stayed aboard the float for five days until he sold the unusual craft for $800.

One day a vessel came into Malacca bearing a Lascar from

the other float. She had steered right before the wind until reaching a small island near the Straits of Malacca where the crew had gone ashore for water. There the Malays attacked the Lascars and murdered them in cold blood. He was the only one who escaped. By stealing a canoe, he reached Rhio, in the Island of Bentang, where he obtained a passage in the ship which carried him to Malacca.

The story of the *Fanny* survivors is indeed unusual. Wrecked on a reef of rocks in the middle of the Chinese Ocean, the *Fanny* was not dashed to pieces at once, but remained together long enough for two floats to be constructed from her hull. More remarkable than anything else, however, is that twenty persons could sail 1,100 miles through tempestuous seas for thirty days in such a makeshift craft to reach her goal. Surely the details of this epic journey rival the voyage of Captain Bligh of *Mutiny on the Bounty* fame.

Mr. Page obtained a passage for the other survivors to Bombay in the *Minerva,* which came into Malacca about twenty days after his own arrival there. He kept a most careful and accurate journal of his experiences, remaining methodical and businesslike to the end. His final page of the report which he made listed the details of what happened to each of the seventy-one persons aboard the *Fanny*. With the list, just as Second Mate Page wrote it more than a century and a half ago, I conclude this chapter:

Killed by the fall of the mast in the typhoon	1
Died at sea	5
Died on the rocks	1
Poisoned himself in the Lascars' float	1
Murdered by the Malays	26
Died of Scurvy in the Europeans' float	1
Washed out of the boat	1
Dead	*36*

The chief mate and his servant went on shore at
Hainan, with four men 6
Ran away with the long-boat 4

Missing   10

Portuguese taken off the rock 4
Landed at Malacca from the float of the Europeans   20
Landed from the Lascars' float 1

Preserved   25

Total   71

WRECKS IN EUROPEAN WATERS

⚓

PART V

WRECKS IN EUROPEAN WATERS

CHAPTER TWENTY-TWO

Mary Rose, Vasa and *Royal George*

⚓

Three great warships sank to the bottom of the ocean under similar circumstances with great loss of life in each case—the *Mary Rose* of England in 1545, the *Vasa* of Sweden in 1628 and the *Royal George* of England in 1782. All three went down by careening so far that their ports were filled with water.

Although attempts were made to bring up each ship from the bottom at the time, none was successful. However, more than three centuries later the Swedish ship, the *Vasa,* was brought to the surface by men with remarkable patience and ingenuity. Long before this time the other two craft had disintegrated. The *Vasa* proved to be in such a fine state of preservation because the *Teredo navales,* which destroys wooden ships underwater, is unable to survive in the Baltic Sea due to the fact that the water is less saline than in the Atlantic Ocean.

The first disaster, 418 years ago, is almost shrouded in antiquity, but I have been able to gather the essential facts concerning the *Mary Rose*. An eyewitness to the sinking, Sir Peter Carewe,* wrote that after the English and the French had fought each other off Spithead, the English Navy came into the harbor. Then the French ships harried the coast, approaching right up to Spithead.

When King Henry VIII heard this, he fretted, "his teeth stood on an edge, to see the bravery of his enemies, to come so near his nose, and he not able to encounter with them."

The king ordered all coastal warning beacons set afire and called out his home guards to stand ready. Next, he ordered all ships to sail to Portsmouth to repel a possible invasion, and left at once to go aboard the *Greate Henry*, then at Spithead.

"The Frenchmen, perceiving that they could do no good by tarrying there, departed again to the seas."

When King Henry arrived, he went out aboard the *Greate Henry*, "and was there served by the Lord Admiral, Sir George Carewe, this gentleman, Peter Carewe, and their uncle, Sir Gawen Carewe; and with such others only as were appointed to that voyage and service. The King, being at dinner, willed some one to go up to the top and see whether he could see anything at the seas."

Three or four ships of the French fleet were then sighted, and King Henry ordered battle stations for everyone. The monarch then went ashore.

Sir George Carewe of the *Mary Rose* went aboard his ship and ordered all hands to battle stations and the sails hoisted at once. The order was scarcely given when the *Mary Rose* began to heel, or lean on one side. She continued to careen

* The details are in *Archeologia*, Volume XXVIII, and are taken from a manuscript which in the year 1847 was in the possession of Sir Thomas Phillip, Bart.

and then began to sink. Of the seven hundred or so aboard, only a handful escaped drowning!

"It chanced," wrote Peter Carewe, "unto this gentleman, as the common proverb is 'the more cooks, the worst potage.' He had in this ship a hundred mariners, the worst of them being able to be the master in the best ship within the realm, and these so maligned and disdained one the other, that refusing to do that which they should do, were careless to do what they ought to do; and so contending in envy, perished in forwardness."

King Henry watched in horror as the great warship slowly sank beneath the waves, and tried to comfort the wife of Sir George Carewe, who was at his side.

Meanwhile 105 ships of the British fleet chased the French fleet over the horizon, without any resistance. Returning to Spithead, several of the ships picked up a handful of survivors, but it was too late for most of the others in the ship's company of the *Mary Rose*.

On July 23, 1545, Lord Russell wrote to Sir William Paget concerning the wreck, and I now quote from the British State Papers (Volume 1, page 793), in which Russell speaks of the *Mary Rose*, which "through such reckeness and great negligence should be in such wise cast away."

Charles, Duke of Suffolk, wrote to Paget on August 1, 1545:

Concerning the Mary Rose, we have consulted and spiken together with them that have taken upon them to recover her, who desireth to have, for the saving of her, such necessaries as is mentioned . . . so that shortly she may be saved. . . . First, two of the greatest hulks that may be gotten; besides the hulks that ride within the haven, four of the greatest hoys within the haven, five of the greatest cables that may be had, ten great hawsers, ten new capstans . . . thirty Venetian mariners, and one Venetian carpenter,—sixty English mariners to attend.

The next day John Viscount Lisle also wrote to Sir William Paget that "the two hulks, the *Jesus of Lubick* . . . and the *Sampson* . . . are brought unto the *Mary Rose,* because they must weigh her up."

On August 7, 1545, the Duke of Suffolk wrote to Paget that the Lord Admiral "had a good hope of the weighing upright of the *Mary Rose* this afternoon or to-morrow."

And so it went through the remainder of 1545, but "this afternoon or to-morrow" never came, and the years and then the centuries went by. An unknown poet of the period shall end our discussion of the unfortunate *Mary Rose:*

There she lay, e'en till this day,
In the deep Bay of St. Helen's O.

In the spring of the year 1628 the new Swedish warship *Vasa,* then in Stockholm Harbor, was moved to the site of the royal palace, where the great task of getting her armament and ballast aboard began. Final loading was completed the first week in August.

On Sunday afternoon, August 10, the *Vasa* was warped from the royal palace against a light breeze to start her first real voyage. Suddenly a squall caught her, and the *Vasa* heeled to port, a bad list developing at once. An attempt was made to haul the cannon to windward counteracting the list, but before this could be done the water poured into the open lower cannon ports making this maneuver impossible. The *Vasa* sank at five o'clock that afternoon, carrying a great number to their death.

Of course, blame was put on the builder, who is said to have constructed the *Vasa* well but with wrong proportions. An opinion could not be obtained from the chief designer of the *Vasa,* Heinrich Hybertsson, because he had passed away the previous year. No one apparently knew why the lower cannon ports were not closed in time, and this point was not brought up at the court of inquiry which followed. Almost everyone had his own theory as to why the *Vasa* sank, but this question may never be fully answered.

Three days after the catastrophe which befell the *Vasa* in Stockholm Harbor, a British engineer named Ian Bulmer was given permission to bring up the wreck. He agreed to salvage the warship with the understanding "no cure, no pay." Working very hard at the bottom of the sea, he managed to raise her to an even keel but went no further. The following year the Royal Swedish Navy attempted to salvage the *Vasa,* but they also failed. Many others have made similar attempts down through the years, but Hans von Treileben was one of those who succeeded. He appeared in the year 1658, anxious to attempt salvaging guns and other material from the warship.

In the year 1663, together with Andreas Peckell, von Treileben began working on the *Vasa.* The diver was dressed in a watertight flexible leather suit and worked from a diving bell with a six-foot boat hook. He actually could communicate to the ship on the surface by pulling a rope in the bell. On April 1, 1664, the divers brought up the first cannon, and by 1665 most of the guns had been recovered. Nothing else was salvaged at this time.

In 1954 Anders Franzen began a systematic search for the *Vasa* and rediscovered her in 110 feet of water almost at the site of the naval dockyard. The *Vasa* Committee was now formed. They reported a plan for the salvage of the entire craft in which the first step would be to lift the ship from 110 feet of water to a depth of 50 feet below the surface, where the ship would remain until further salvage plans were worked out.

In August 1959, the initial raising of the *Vasa* began. In eighteen stages workmen moved her 1,500 feet to a location near Kastellholmen, where she remained at a depth of 50 feet of water. The project was completed by September 1959. In April 1961, a large salvage armada arrived over the wreck, and four pontoons were inflated to a lifting capacity of five tons each. Hydraulic jacks now brought the hull close to the surface, and on April 24 the superstructure of the ancient warship broke surface. Powerful salvage pumps were brought right on board the *Vasa* at this time.

By May 4, 1961, the world's oldest identifiable ship was afloat. She was brought into the King Gustaf V dry dock at Beckholmen, where a large raft made of concrete had already been submerged at the bottom of the dock. This concrete raft will serve through the years as the floor of the *Vasa* Museum, for she is now on exhibition, and people from all over the world come to see her at her unusual location in Stockholm Harbor known as the *Vasa* Dockyard.

Mr. John R. Herbert, editor of the *Patriot Ledger* in Quincy, Massachusetts, visited the *Vasa* in Stockholm Harbor during the summer of 1962 and was impressed with the progress which had been made on the ship since she was brought up from the bottom of the sea. His remarks follow:

The *Vasa* is located a short distance from downtown Stockholm in a building of aluminum. It is a specially developed site, called Vasavarvet, which means the *Vasa* drydock. The ship itself is sitting on a floating concrete pontoon and the entire craft is in a covered aluminum building so as to make the humidification, which is always turned on, practical.

Reconstruction is always going on, but how far this reconstruction will go is a matter still under discussion.

Visitors may see the ship from two different balconies or levels. One balcony is about 20 feet higher than the other. The lower balcony gives the visitor the picture at the water line. The upper balcony is arranged so that you can look down on the vessel. No one is allowed to go aboard, because there is a constant spraying of water and chemicals and it is quite messy.

In addition to the ship itself, Vasavarvet has an office building, two stores, a theater, a restaurant, and a museum. The *Vasa* itself is right at the edge of Stockholm Harbor. Parking facilities are on the other side of the collection of buildings. The *Vasa* is now the greatest tourist attraction in all Sweden.

Complete reconstruction will take a great many years. The *Vasa* presently constitutes the world's largest jigsaw puzzle. All the pieces are present, but the puzzle is how to put them together.

In 1782, 154 years after the sinking of the *Vasa,* another warship suffered disaster in similar fashion, this time in England.

She was the *Royal George.* Again, the sudden manner in which she was lost has prevented any really accurate story of the accident from ever being published.

At the time of the disaster which drowned so many hundreds of men and women, the *Royal George* was the oldest first-rate warship in the British service. She was built at Woolwich, where her keel was laid in 1751. According to the custom of the period she was hauled out of dock in July 1755, as large ships were not built on slips to launch. Pierced for one hundred guns, she afterward had two additional ports, so that including carronades she mounted 108 guns. She was rather short and high, but still she was an excellent sailer and made a fine record between the years 1756 and 1782.

Lord Anson, Admiral Boscawen, Lord Rodney, Lord Howe and many others served as commanders of the *Royal George* in this period. Lawke commanded her in the squadron which defeated the French under Conflans, when the *Superbe,* of seventy guns, was sunk by her cannon. She also was responsible for the sixty-four-gun man-of-war *Soleil Royale*'s being driven on shore and burned.

The *Royal George* carried the tallest masts and squarest canvas of any English-built ship in the navy, as well as the heaviest metal, including fifty-two, forty and twenty-eight pounders. They were afterward changed on account of her age to forty, thirty-two and eighteen pounders.

The *Royal George* had just returned from a cruise, so that she had more water in her hold than usual. As the water did not decrease after she came into harbor, an order was issued on Saturday, August 14, 1782, for her to go into dock. A strict survey by the carpenter and others was made before she entered dry dock, and they found the leak was not more than two feet below the watermark. Therefore, it was resolved, in order to save time, that she should be laid down at Spithead and heeled over for repairs. Meanwhile, it was discovered that the pipe which occasionally admitted the water to cleanse and sweeten the ship was out of order and that it was necessary to replace it with a new one.

Thus the problem which presented itself became more complicated, because the *Royal George* had to be heeled over at a greater angle to expose the water pipe. Most of the guns were removed from one side to the other. The actual heeling now began, but when the *Royal George* was careened she did not stop until her list was ten degrees more than planned. As in the case of the *Vasa* 154 years earlier, the crew had forgotten to stop the scuppers on the lower decks, allowing the water to pour into the ship. At the moment most of the crew were at dinner, but the carpenters and caulkers continued working.

Almost finished with their repairs, the workmen were about to lay down their tools when a squall took the ship on the raised side, and the lower deck ports to leeward being open, the water rushed in. As soon as the crew discovered their dangerous situation, they beat the signal "to arms" so that they could right the ship, but their efforts were in vain.

In less than eight minutes she fell flat on one side, rapidly filling with water. The guns, shot and other heavy material falling from the other side accelerated her descent, and she went to the bottom so rapidly that the officers, in their confusion, made no signal of distress, nor, indeed, could anyone have helped them if they had, for after her lower ports were in the water, no power on earth could have prevented her from going to the bottom.

At this fatal moment there were nearly 1,200 persons on board, including about 250 women and children, relatives of the seamen. Their families had been permitted to visit the ship and were allowed to remain on board until the order arrived for her sailing. Most of the watch on deck, amounting to about 230 sailors, were saved by the boats which the ships lying nearby had manned and sent to the distress area. Rescue work had to be delayed until the whirlpool caused by the sudden sinking of the vessel subsided. Then the boats picked up seventy more men who floated to the surface one by one after the ship had disappeared. Saved in this manner were four lieutenants, eleven women and fifty-five seamen.

Among the officers rescued from the brink of eternity was Lieutenant Durham, officer of the watch on deck at the time when the vessel started going down. He had just time to throw off his coat and scramble onto a beam, from which he was soon washed. A moment later he found himself floating about among men and hammocks. A drowning marine caught him by the waistcoat and clutched him in such a deathlike grasp that he was drawn underwater three different times. In vain he reasoned with the man who still clung to him desperately. Finally, unbuttoning his waistcoat and twisting his shoulders, he slid out from both the garment and the grasp of the dying marine, who sank at once.

Lieutenant Durham then climbed to the top rigging, which was still above the surface. Declining help when a lifeboat came by, he told the rescuers to save Captain Waghorne, who was in immediate danger of drowning. After the captain had been saved, Durham was taken up and conveyed safely to the shore.

Mr. Henry Bishop, a young man of about nineteen, was saved in a most extraordinary manner. On the lower deck at the time of the fatal accident, Bishop was driven by the seas up the hatchway at the same instant that one of the cannons fell from the middle deck, striking him on his left hand. In a few seconds he found himself floating on the surface of the water and before long was taken up by one of the boats. Later he found that the cannon had broken three of his fingers.

Nearly nine hundred persons lost their lives in the disaster. Among them was Admiral Kempenfelt, whose career in the navy had been a glorious one. His flag was flying in 1781 on board the *Royal George*, then part of Lord Howe's fleet.

Besides the admiral, who was in his cabin writing on his plan for improving signal systems when the sudden disaster happened, everyone who was between decks perished with the warship. Captain Waghorne, the admiral's first captain, was fortunately on deck, but his son, who was a lieutenant on board, was lost. This disastrous accident drowned a multitude of gallant men, many of them with their wives and families in the very midst of a period of happiness which they were enjoying to the utmost. There they were, anchored on their own coast, in fair weather and in smooth water. Nevertheless, in a moment they were overwhelmed by the ocean which poured tons and tons of water in around them, engulfing entire families forever. A great number of those who struggled to the surface were saved by going out on the topsail yards, which remained above water after the ship reached the bottom.

Every effort was made by the boats of the rest of the fleet to save the crew, and they were able to pick up Captain Waghorne, a few officers and about three hundred people. As the vessel was lying at Spithead, it happened that scores of the seamen and some of the officers had gone ashore, while, on the other hand, a great many women and children were on board. A large sum of money was raised by subscription for the relief of the widows, children and relatives of those who perished by this fatal accident.

The masts of the *Royal George* remained standing for a considerable time afterward. As the years went by, much of the hull was exposed at low water, but a few decades after the terrible disaster, the wreck became covered with sand and was no longer visible.

Rear Admiral Kempenfelt was the son of Lieutenant Colonel Kempenfelt, a native of Sweden, whose excellent character was highly esteemed.* Young Kempenfelt took part in the capture of Portobello and had worked his way up to the rank of admiral, which position he achieved in 1780. In 1781 he gained a brilliant victory over the French near Ushant. Admiral Kempenfelt was trapped aboard the *Royal George* when his cabin door jammed, and he was drowned with the others. His loss was a severe one to the British Navy.

On September 9, 1782, a court-martial was held at Portsmouth on board the *Warspite,* concerning the loss of the *Royal George.* After an examination of such imperfect evidence as could be obtained, Captain Waghorne was honorably acquitted. A carpenter on board who had escaped

---

* Colonel Kempenfelt was depicted and immortalized by Joseph Addison in the *Spectator,* where he has ever been admired under the well-known appellation of Captain Sentry. Lieutenant Colonel Kempenfelt followed the fortunes of King James the Second, and was afterward invited by Queen Anne to accept a commission in her service: he died while lieutenant governor of Jersey, during the reign of George the First. The colonel left two sons and two daughters, none of whom was ever married. One of the sons, Gustavus Adolphus Kempenfelt, Esq., was a captain in the army; the other, Richard Kempenfelt, Esq., the admiral, was born in Westminster, and soon discovering uncommon talents for the profession of the navy, he entered very early into the service.

declared that the ship sank so suddenly that he had only time to tell his brother that he was sinking, and down she went. It also appeared that the ship was so old and in so unseaworthy a condition that when a plank started not a peg would hold together. The belief has come up through the years that when the water poured in, her entire bottom on the starboard side ripped off.

On the day that the court-martial was held, the body of Bruce Saunders, the first lieutenant, was taken up under the stern of the *Montague,* East Indiaman, at the Motherbank. His gold watch was in his fob,* and the sum of five pounds, fifteen shillings and sixpence was found in his pocket.

I now quote from the pen of a survivor of the disaster:

The water-cock ought to have been put to rights before the shot was put on board. It is my opinion, that had the lieutenant of the watch given orders, to "right ship," when the carpenter first spoke to him, nothing amiss would have happened, as three or four men at each tackle of the starboard guns would very soon have bowsed the guns all out, and by so doing have righted the ship.

At the time this happened, the vessel was anchored by two anchors from the head. The wind was from the north-west, only a trifling breeze; and there was now, a sudden gust of wind which made her heel just before she sunk; it was, I felt convinced, the weight of metal and water which rushed in at the port-holes, that sunk her, and not the effects of the wind upon her. She had not even a stitch of canvass to keep her head steady as she lay at anchor; she had six months' provisions on board, and many tons of shot.

The water-cock, the cause of all this fearful loss of life, is preserved in Portsmouth Dock-yard; a memorial of a second man-of-war overset at Spithead, through neglect and careless-

---

* A little pocket in men's trousers near the waistband.

ness. The first being the *Marye Rose,* cast away near the same spot, in the reign of Henry the Eighth.

We trust sincerely that whilst the "neglect and carelessness" of which he speaks will ever be remembered with deep regret by every Englishman, it will serve as a warning to future generations and prevent a recurrence of so fearful a catastrophe. Thus we must realize that all of us should be ever vigilant whether out on the ocean, in sight of land or even within the "fancied security of some friendly port."

Many British scientists were interested in bringing the guns and cannon of the *Royal George* to the surface. A diving bell was built, and on the twenty-first of November, 1782, sixteen guns and much cordage were raised. Shortly afterward, by the ingenuity of a salvage group of Braithwaite and Sons, the mainsheet anchor of the *Royal George* was safely delivered into the King's yard, Portsmouth. At the time it was believed to be the heaviest in the world, weighing 9,800 pounds. By means of Braithwaite's diving bell, the men could work underwater for several hours together, and they had entertained hopes of being able to weigh the vessel, but all their attempts for this purpose proved unsuccessful. Several attempts have been made at different times and by various constructions, some of which were attended with no success, others with very little, and in more than one instance human life has been sacrificed to the experiments.

The following spring, a monument was erected in the churchyard at Portsea to the memory of the brave, unfortunate Admiral Kempenfelt and his fellow sufferers, who perished in the *Royal George.*

It can be said without fear of contradiction that diving and salvage work really began at Spithead on the wreck of the *Royal George.* Sixty-five feet down, the hull had hit the bottom, but the top of her masts still were above the surface. The Admirality now attempted to raise her, setting up a cradle of cables between two ships, but this maneuver failed completely. As late as 1799, and possibly later, her mainmasts showed stiff and erect above the water at Spithead.

Gunpowder was placed aboard and exploded. Divers attempting to recover material had only partial success. Finally in 1839 Colonel Charles Pasley, of the Army's Royal Sappers,* arrived on the scene with a diving bell. He brought along four officers, twenty-three sappers and nine men, all soldiers. The diving bell plan failed completely. Pasley now experimented with diving suits. Two failed, but the third, an invention of Augustus Siebe, was successful.

It was now the year 1840 and fifty-seven years had elapsed. The *Royal George* had been taken over by the elements, which reduced the wreck to a mere hulk. Many of the guns had broken through the sides and were embedded in silt and mud. Colonel Pasley exploded several barrels of gunpowder against the hull of the ship. Some objects brought up at the time included a dog collar inscribed "Thomas Little, HMS *Victory* 1781," a musket and a human skull.

Lance Corporal Richard P. Jones was probably the best diver to go down on the wreck of the *Royal George*. One day when the visibility was practically zero he encountered a smooth object half afloat off the deck. He felt a type of grating and suddenly realized that he was counting the vertebrae of a drowned human body. It was a terrible experience and it was some time before Jones took another dive.

Diving continued off and on for the next few years, but nothing else of importance ever transpired. A painting of the disaster is in the Royal United Service Institution at London, and William Cowper's famous poem commemorates the event:

* A military engineer.

ON THE LOSS OF THE *Royal George*

Toll for the brave!
　The brave that are no more!
All sunk beneath the wave,
　Fast by their native shore!

Eight hundred of the brave,
　Whose courage well was tried,
Had made the vessel heel,
　And lay her on her side.

Toll for the brave!
　Brave Kempenfelt is gone;
His last sea-fight is fought;
　His work of glory done.

But Kempenfelt is gone,
　His victories are o'er;
And he and his eight hundred
　Shall plough the wave no more.

CHAPTER TWENTY-THREE

The *Ajax*

⚓

On the night of February 14, 1807, the seventy-four-gun man-of-war *Ajax,* commanded by Captain Henry Blackwood, lay at anchor off the mouth of the Dardanelles.* She was in company with the squadron of Vice Admiral John Duckworth. The wind, which during the day was boisterous, had fallen. In the clear moonlight every object was visible with a distinctness almost equal to that of day.

The scene from the deck of the *Ajax* was one of beauty, with bright moonbeams on the waters leaving a silvery track. Ahead and astern, the high masts of the other squadron ships tapered toward the sky, with the outline of every rope and spar sharply defined against the firmament.

Soon after nine o'clock in the evening, Captain Blackwood

* The Dardanelles are between the Balkan Peninsula in Europe and Asia Minor, and lead from the Aegean Sea into the Sea of Marmara, the Bosporus and the Black Sea.

received from his first lieutenant the usual report that all was
well aboard. Everyone, except those on duty, had retired to
his berth. A very short time had elapsed, however, before the
stillness of that night was broken by the appalling cry of
"Fire!"

The officer of the watch instantly informed Captain Blackwood of the situation. The captain hastened up on deck, and
found flames bursting from the afterdeck. He then directed
Lieutenant Wood and a midshipman to proceed in one of
the boats to all the ships of the squadron to request assistance.
It was a moment of horror for Blackwood. His ship and six
hundred men were threatened with immediate destruction,
and each man looked to him for direction and guidance.

Followed by several of his officers, the captain went down
to the cockpit where the smoke was belching forth. The men
fought desperately to put out the flames in that part of the
ship, but the blaze gained rapidly, and it soon was impossible
to remain below. Several of the men in the bucket brigade
fainted from suffocation with the buckets in their hands. To
get more air the lower-deck ports were hauled up, but this
increased the density of the smoke. Immediately they were
closed again and the after-hatchway was shut down. The carpenter went below to try to scuttle the afterpart of the ship,
but after a desperate effort he failed completely and was
forced to abandon his attempt.

Ten minutes after the first alarm had been given the flames
raged out of control. Luckily, the captain had ordered the
jolly boat lowered when he first went up on deck. The flames
now burst up the main hatchway, dividing the fore from the
after part of the ship, and the captain ordered all hands to
the forecastle. Realizing that the *Ajax* was doomed, he told
every man to look out for himself.

Wrapped in flames from amidships to taffrail, the ship
soon became the scene of utmost horror. Hundreds of hu-

mans, crowded close together on the forecastle and bowsprit, were faced with that most terrible of all ocean calamities, fire at sea. No other boat had yet come to their assistance, as Lieutenant Wood had hardly reached the first warship to get help. The situation leveled all rank; men and officers huddled together, watching the fire gain and feeling the heat from the holocaust slowly mount.

The spectacle of the mighty *Ajax* ablaze from stem to stern was watched by hundreds of sailors on the other ships of the squadron in silent awe. Volumes of black smoke rose in huge pillars from all parts of the vessel, but far above the hissing and crackling of the flames as they leaped up the masts and rigging came the shrieks and death yells of scores upon scores of helpless men who had climbed aloft. Some, rather than stand the horrible suspense, plunged overboard, where they ended their lives and sufferings in a watery grave. Now began the booming of the guns of the *Ajax*. As they exploded they echoed far and wide over the waters, adding to the terror of that awful night.

The other boats could soon be seen approaching the stricken ship. Standing on the blazing forecastle in the midst of his men, Captain Blackwood cried out to them to keep up their courage just a little longer, as the rescue craft would soon come. The brave captain climbed over the gunwale and leaped into the sea. He managed to stay afloat until he was picked up by the first boat, which was from the *Canopus*, another ship of the fleet.

Finally the boats from the squadron arrived in great numbers. While the survivors were being rescued, the agonizing cries of the sufferers were changed into wild shouts of joy as the men were pulled to safety. Unfortunately, so many of the crew had jumped into the sea that it was impossible for the boats to pick them all up, and countless numbers drowned.

Lieutenant Nisbit Willoughby of the *St. George* hastened in a cutter to assist those in the water, and soon the cutter was packed with survivors. Many had to be left behind to ensure the safety of those in the overladen boat, but fortunately, some launches and a barge arrived in time to pick up the remainder and convey them to the different ships of the squadron.

All this time the blazing *Ajax* was drifting toward the island of Tenedos. Swinging in the light breeze which had come up, she presented her stern and broadside alternately to the wind. Meanwhile Lieutenant Willoughby had made two trips, and his boat was almost filled for the third time when he observed several men hanging by the ropes under the head of the *Ajax*, as she slowly swung around.

The dramatic spectacle so impressed him that he resolved at all hazards to rescue the men, and running in under the blazing bow, he got them aboard the cutter. Suddenly the wind caught the *Ajax* against the cutter, which was trapped across the man-of-war's hawse * in the path of flames roaring out of the hull.

For Willoughby to extricate himself from this perilous situation was almost impossible, for every moment increased the speed of with which the *Ajax* was surging through the water, and she threatened to ride right over his small boat destroying it in an instant.

Quoting from a writer of the period:

Whilst the *Ajax* was propelling the cutter in the above alarming manner, the flames reached the shank, painter and stopper, of her remaining bower anchor, and it fell from her bows, nearly effecting the destruction of the boat at its first plunge into the water. The cable caught her outer gunwale,

* The hawse is that part of a ship's bows in which the hawse-holes are cut for the cables to pass through.

over which it ran, apparently one sheet of fire; orders, exertion and presence of mind were now of no avail. Death to all in the cutter appeared inevitable.

The boats at a distance saw that the cutter was enveloped in flames, and therefore considered it impossible to assist her. All that Lieutenant Willoughby and his companions could do while the cable was running out was to keep the sparks and flames as much as possible from the uncovered parts of their persons. Providentially, although the inner portion of the cable had been burnt through, the anchor took the ground, and gave the ship's head a check to windward, before the less consumed part had entirely left the tier; and thus the very event which had seemed to seal the doom of the cutter was in all respects ordained by the Almighty for her preservation. The change in the ship's position enabled the boat to get clear, but not before every individual in her was more or less severely scorched.

The wreck drifted onto the shore on the north side of the island of Tenedos, where, at five o'clock in the morning, she blew up with an explosion which must have been felt for miles around, and all that remained of the *Ajax* were a few smoking spars.

Such was the fate of this great ship, destroyed by a conflagration more rapid than had ever been known. The real cause of the blaze is still a mystery. It appears that there had been a light in the bread room, contrary to orders, and the fire probably started there because of someone's carelessness.

"I trust," said Captain Blackwood, in his defense months later before the inevitable court of inquiry, "that I shall be able to prove to the satisfaction of this court that I had instituted a regulation which obliged the first lieutenant, the warrant officers and master at arms, in a body to visit all the quarters. I trust this court will consider that in ordering the first lieutenant and warrant officers to visit all parts of the ship, whose report, as well as that of the master at arms, I had received at a few minutes past eight o'clock, I had very fully provided for every want, and might with perfect confidence have considered my ship in a state of perfect safety with respect to fire."

Captain Blackwood, his surviving officers and men, were all most honorably acquitted of any blame respecting the loss of the *Ajax*. Out of 600 men, 350 were saved by the boats of the squadron; but 250 perished that night by burning to death or drowning.

CHAPTER TWENTY-FOUR

The Steamer *Killarney*

⚓

When the 200-ton steamer *Killarney* left Cork for Bristol, England, on Friday morning January 19, 1838, there were 21 passengers on board, 22 in the crew, 100 tons of goods and 650 pigs, part of which were in the hold and the remainder carried on the deck of the steamer.

Soon after Captain George Bailley took the *Killarney* out of the harbor a gale struck the steamer. First Mate George Rowles reported that the great number of pigs on the deck caused her to develop an unusual roll and pitch and she started to ship seas. The passengers began to show alarm and soon prevailed on Captain Bailley to put back into port. The *Killarney* reversed her course and returned to Cork.

By evening the wind moderated, and Captain Bailley resumed his voyage. The vessel had scarcely left the harbor a second time, however, when the wind rose violently again, increasing until it blew a gale. To make matters worse a heavy fog now set in, which continued all night long, and the vessel rolled in terrible fashion. One sea poured into the hold, the hatches having been left open in order to get enough air to the pigs.

The captain now asked every person on board to help throw the animals overboard, as those on deck crowded the lee side of the vessel. This was almost impossible to do, however, and only a few were tossed into the sea. The waves continued to wash over the deck and drench the hold. The pumps worked successfully in ridding the hold of the water until four o'clock Saturday morning when some small coal got into them and choked them. The water then rose rapidly until it reached the level of the fire in the boiler, which it extinguished, and the engine no longer moved. A bucket brigade was organized, with everyone aboard joining in the line. Working for their very lives, the men gained so effectively against the water that the boiler fire could be lighted again.

Unfortunately, because of the fog, they did not even know where they were or the direction they were taking. The crew tried to keep the vessel's head to the wind, but, after some time, they found they were going to leeward. The jibsail was set in order to keep her steady, but no sooner was it run out than it was blown into ribbons.

About three o'clock the fog cleared away, and they saw land behind them. However, no one could tell with certainty what part of the coast it was. It was then blowing a complete hurricane, and the opposite shore was covered with rocks. If they drifted toward land, destruction was inevitable. The mainsail was set, and the captain shouted to the engineer to build up steam in order to keep her off the rocks. The steam, unfortunately, was so weak as to be of no assistance, for it scarcely moved the crank. The sail now had to be hauled down lest it throw the *Killarney* on her beam ends. The staysail was then tried in the hope that it would enable them to round the point, but the wind blew so fiercely they could not haul it out.

Meanwhile they were drifting nearer and nearer a huge rock some distance from shore. Just as they had succeeded in getting her before the wind, she was struck by a tremendous sea which carried away the taffrail, the wheel and the two men who worked it. Fortunately the men caught part of the rigging and were saved; but the sea carried away the bulwarks with some of the steerage passengers who were standing near the funnel and at once cleared the deck of all the pigs.

The steward now went down to call the cabin passengers on deck. They were on their way up when a sea passed over the vessel. A second wave struck almost immediately, and scarcely had two of the passengers stepped on the quarter-deck than they were swept overboard. These two seas had the effect of bringing the head of the vessel around to windward again. A third wave caught the *Killarney* and drove her with great force onto the gigantic boulder. It was then between four and five o'clock.

The carpenter jumped on the great rock, followed by one of the passengers, but the landing place was so narrow that the passenger soon slipped off into the water and drowned.

After striking, the vessel broke free. She soon hit again, however, and continued falling off and striking for some time, during which some of the sailors, the mate and Captain Bailley landed. When the captain got on the rock, a rope was thrown to him and the mate so that they might try to keep the vessel secured. Most of the sailors and some of the passengers were saved by jumping to the rock and then going ashore one at a time.

Before leaving the vessel, the steward scrambled along the deck to look for one of the women, a Mrs. Lawe. He found her near the funnel, calm and collected. With some difficulty he brought her to the quarter-gallery. Grabbing the rope, he handed it to her, directing her to take hold of it and, when the vessel next struck, to leap into the sea. Then they would drag her to the rock. She did so, and was drawn up part of the way, but suddenly her strength failed and she let go the rope. A great wave swept over her, and she was never seen again.

The steward leaped almost at the same moment and was saved. The last persons who left the vessel were a sailor and the unconscious stewardess, whom the sailor held in his arms. He jumped from the vessel and reached the rock holding the woman under one arm all the time. The footing was narrow, and the rock shelving. Since he had room for little more than his toes, he tried to hold on with the fingers of one hand, but the weight of the woman pulled him backwards. They fell into the sea and were both drowned.

One of the passengers, a physician, had his little son in his arms and was comforting him. When the vessel struck, he flung the lad with all his strength toward the rock. The child reached the lower part of it in safety, though the violence of the effort had nearly carried the father overboard. Reaching the rock himself, the doctor took the child in his arms, and by hugging him closely, tried to keep the boy warm. Suddenly he looked up at his father.

"Kiss me," said the lad, "we'll meet no more!" The next moment he slipped down the rock and into the ocean, and was soon swallowed up by the raging waves.

The next sea now drove the *Killarney* high against the boulder, tearing open her deck. She broke in two, fore and aft, with everyone on board perishing. An hour later, except for the engine and paddle wheel, nothing of the vessel or her machinery remained in sight.

About twenty-five persons were now on the huge rock. The sailors had crawled around to the sheltered side, but the passengers were not so fortunate. One man, wearing only his shirt and vest, was seated astride a projection of the rock, his face toward the sea. Close by, below him, was another man, his back to the sea, his toes resting on a narrow ledge, his fingers clinging to a crevice. All around them others were equally exposed and helpless.

The sailors facing land could see a group of people on shore walking at the top of a cliff. Shouting across to attract their attention, the men received no answer. As they learned later, at that time they were neither seen nor heard. The sailors noticed that the people were carrying off some of the pigs which had washed ashore, but by late afternoon the shore was again deserted.

The unfortunate survivors now faced a long night of suffering. Late that afternoon a wind came up, which became cold and bitter by midnight and blew with great fury. Every so often there was a terrible shriek, heard even above the wild gale then blowing, as one after another lost his hold and slipped down the side of the rock and into the sea.

When morning came the survivors clambered to the sheltered side of their refuge, where they noticed that men were waving across to them from the cliff. Desperate attempts were made to save them, but as the storm continued, those ashore could not reach them. Several heavy beams with ropes firmly fastened to them and to the shore were floated out to the rock when the tide turned and started to go out, but only one reached the vicinity, and that the sufferers were unable to secure in time. Wire was then attached to bullets, which were shot out to the rock, with rope attached to the wire, but the efforts ended unsuccessfully.

Darkness settled down that terrible Sunday shortly after the last attempt failed, and soon those on the rock could not see the figures of people high above them on the cliff. They now became convinced that they had little time left to live.

Their only food and drink for the two previous days and

nights since they had left the wreck had been salt water mixed with rain and seaweed. That night, nevertheless, was not so severe, and at daylight the cliffs were crowded with people, all anxious to help rescue the sufferers out on the rock.

On Monday morning Captain Manby's lifesaving apparatus was taken by cart to the top of the cliff, but the shot and rope still did not reach the survivors. Other efforts were made at the time, none of which was successful. Then the cannon was moved to a lower level nearer the rock, and a line was fired directly across. It was secured at once by the survivors, and at eleven o'clock two loaves of bread and a little wine and spirits were lowered to the sufferers, the first real food they had had since Friday.

After refreshing themselves, they were told to get ready to be hauled off. A short time later the first sailor grabbed the lines and was pulled aloft. One by one the members of the crew and the passengers were transferred to the top of the cliff until all had been saved.

Of the forty-three persons who embarked on Friday morning, only thirteen escaped alive, and of the thirteen, one died soon after he was rescued.

CHAPTER TWENTY-FIVE

The Strange Voyage of the *Vryheid*

In the year 1802 a Dutch ship named *Vryheid* was desperately needed by the Netherlands government for the purpose of carrying troops to Batavia in the East Indies, where the Dutch had been developing the northern part of Java for many generations.*

The *Vryheid* was formerly the *Melville Castle,* a veteran ship of the British East India Company. Unfortunately, she had been sold to the merchants of Amsterdam only after her real worth as a sailing craft was at an end. Nevertheless, as the Dutch were badly in need of sailing vessels, the *Vryheid* was taken to Amsterdam where she was supposedly repaired and repainted from stem to stern. Finally she was declared in "perfect" condition for the long voyage to Batavia.

* Taken by General Coen of the Netherlands in 1619, Batavia went through various degrees of prosperity, and was only beginning to flourish about the time that the Dutch organized the Batavian Republic, May 16, 1795.

Of course, in order that the venerable hulk be declared ready for sea, corners had been cut, red tape slashed and inspections either glossed over or not made at all. By the first of November a representative of the East India Company declared her to be fit, and the loading of stores began.

The master chosen for the *Vryheid* was Captain Scherman, a mariner with a long record of successful voyages. Unfortunately, he was ill-advised in the ways of men, ships and the sea. If he had made a proper inspection of the *Vryheid* when he took command on November 15, the ship probably would never have left port at all, but the appearance of the new paint on the vessel misled him. His superiors had so impressed Captain Scherman with the necessity of getting the troops to Batavia as fast as possible that he made up his mind to sail through fair and foul weather until their arrival at the island of Java on the other side of the world.

And so it was that early in the morning of November 21, 1802, the *Vryheid* sailed away from Amsterdam. Aboard were 322 soldiers, 42 officers, 22 wives and 7 children of the officers, 28 regular passengers and 61 seamen. The admiral of the Dutch fleet and the colonel of the regiment were also making the long journey.

At first the *Vryheid* appeared to handle well, but when a strong gale started to blow early the next morning, the vessel was shaken repeatedly and began to pitch and stagger.

Captain Scherman, because of his lack of knowledge concerning the ship's actual condition, could not understand how a craft in presumably perfect shape could show such glaring signs of weakness as she was exhibiting. True, the gale was a strong one, but in no sense could it be considered as violent as the straining and staggering of the *Vryheid* indicated. Scherman had often sailed without trouble through stanch blows worse than the one the *Vryheid* was attempting to weather.

Finally the creaking and groaning of the unhappy craft convinced the captain that he should reduce sail, and he ordered the topgallantmasts and the yards struck. For a time, this allowed the *Vryheid* to ride more easily. Then, as noon approached, the wind rose in intensity, and the ship again became unmanageable.

By now many were beginning to fear for their safety, and scores were hopeful that Captain Scherman would return to port. The helplessness of the women was especially distressing to the men, who watched the mothers embracing their children, silently weeping as they attempted to comfort them. Finally the women decided to concentrate their efforts on the captain's wife, who was aboard with her three-month-old baby. The mothers implored Mrs. Scherman to make her husband understand that he should turn back to Amsterdam. The attempt failed, however, and eventually the captain had to force the unhappy women out of his cabin to restore some semblance of discipline.

By three o'clock in the afternoon, the storm grew much worse. A short time later, without warning, the great mainmast crashed into the sea and in its fall swept several crew members overboard to their death. This loss in the moderate gale then blowing completely bewildered Scherman. He could not understand why a recently inspected ship should suffer such damage. Of course, he reasoned, ships lost masts during times of extremely violent storms, but the captain knew instinctively that a mast in first-class condition should not have broken off and fallen into the sea in the disturbance they were then weathering.

Soon the *Vryheid* was off the shores of Kent. Although objects along the coast could easily be seen, the waves were so high that lifeboats from shore could not put off to help. The captain ordered distress guns fired each minute to attract attention from shore, but they went unanswered, so distress flags were hoisted aloft. Again there was no response from land.

When a lull developed a short time later, Captain Scherman was able to anchor at the entrance to Hythe Bay, England. Great billows continued to rush by the *Vryheid*, and darkness fell without any prospect of assistance.

All night long the ship swung at anchor, and around midnight rum was served to the crew. A contemporary chronicler tells us that "a beam of hope illuminated every countenance." Unfortunately, it was of short duration, as ten minutes later a frightened sailor from below rushed up with the report that the so-called first-rate hull had sprung a bad leak. All hands were ordered to the pumps, but before satisfactory progress could be made, the storm returned with renewed energy.

Captain Scherman visited the hold and found the answer to all the trouble. He discovered that the new paint concealed decaying timbers, and he now realized that the mast must have tumbled down because of dry rot concealed in it. The same affliction had visited the planking in the hold. Wrenched free by the storm, the rotting wood allowed the water to pour into the vessel.

A definite list to port soon developed, which added to the terror of the women and children. At dawn the anchor cable snapped, and the *Vryheid* began to drift toward Dymchurch Wall, three miles west of Hythe. The crew could do nothing but continue to fire distress guns and keep their signals flying during the next few hours.

All along the coast people were watching the battered ship as she was being pushed by the gale. At daybreak a pilot boat was put out from Dover, and during a temporary lull in the storm the captain brought his craft alongside the *Vryheid*. Shouting across, he recommended that Captain Scherman sail into either Deal or Hythe to await the storm's end.

"If you proceed," said the pilot boat captain, "all hands

will be lost. Evidently you are unacquainted with the coast. If the gale continues, no power on earth can save you!"

Now that he had help and advice, the *Vryheid's* master chose to ignore both. Instead of accepting the suggestions of the pilot, he listened patiently but made no decision. Disgusted, the pilot finally turned away and sailed back to Dover.

The *Vryheid* continued to drift along off the English coast. A short time later the harbor master at Deal sent out two pilot boats to advise the captain to seek shelter in the nearest harbor. Again the captain listened patiently and took no action.

The gale now began in terrible earnestness, and as they sailed away the two boats fired warning cannons. Still Scherman stubbornly ignored them. Five minutes later both pilot boats headed back toward Deal Harbor. This attitude of Captain Scherman's in the face of danger confused and angered all aboard.

The *Vryheid's* drift continued along the coast. Even then the captain could have ordered the ship's course changed so that he could seek the shelter of the sung harbor, but he refused to consider this plan. Evidently he decided that he would be able to continue drifting offshore until the storm ended when he would make a jury rig or temporary mainmast and proceed to his destination.

A short time after the two boats were out of sight, the gale came back with added strength, and Scherman slowly came to realize that he had lost his foolhardy gamble with the lives of more than four hundred people. Soon the *Vryheid* was battered toward land, a lee shore in the area of the dreaded Dymchurch Wall. The coast, for a stretch of two miles, had been protected from the encroachment of the sea by the placing of immense pilings and overlaths to which were connected long jetties stretching far out into the sea.

On drifted the helpless ship. Nearer and nearer she approached the wooden piling jetties. Soon she was in the trough of giant billows just off the first jetty. Across on the sea wall the English inhabitants were watching an overwhelmingly awesome sight, which they were now powerless to prevent. The people on shore knew that the fate of almost everyone aboard the transport was sealed and that few would survive off the shores of the infamous Dymchurch area.

Soon a great towering wave with a breaking crest roared in toward the *Vryheid,* caught the doomed ship in its grasp, and carried her swiftly toward the wooden barrier just offshore. A moment later, with a splintering of timbers, the ship crashed into the wooden jetty. Her last voyage had come to a tragic end.

In this desperate situation, with the vessel hung up on the jetty and the wind increasing in velocity, the captain finally ordered the mizzenmast to be cut away, and it fell into the sea. It was a moment of terror. Several of the crew, under the direction of the officers, were desperately pumping water from the hold, while another group began throwing the ship's ballast overboard. In spite of everything, the danger increased. So angry were the frightened officers at the captain's refusal to accept help that they openly denounced him. Now that it was too late to do anything about it Scherman admitted his error to the admiral. Breaking down, he explained that he had been anxious to make a success of the voyage in spite of all obstacles. The admiral now suggested that the sheet anchor be cut away, and it was done at once.

The unfortunate ship continued to beat upon the piles, and the sea soon broke over her with such violence that the men were unable to remain in the hold. Completely clogged with sand and mud, the pumps proved totally useless, and a speedy destruction of the vessel and all on board appeared certain.

Soon afterward the foremast crashed over the ship's side,

carrying along with it twelve of the crew who were soon swallowed up by the waves. Several of the women were taken to the bowsprit, where they and their husbands huddled. Others chose to wait their fate on the quarter-deck with Captain Scherman, who stood there in silent despair. His unfortunate wife, in bitterness and anguish, was clinging with her baby as best she could to the captain's feet.

About eight o'clock in the morning the rudder broke off. The tiller began to tear up the gundeck, and the water rushed in through the portholes. At this moment almost every one of the passengers and crew knelt on the sloping deck in solemn prayer to the Almighty. In the midst of the prayer a great wave breached completely over them, and they were forced to interrupt their service to grasp lines and parts of the ship to prevent being swept into the sea. Although the signal guns were fired from time to time, there was little hope of getting help from shore. Wave after wave smashed the ship against the piles with irresistible force.

The long night finally ended, and dawn revealed that the ship was not more than four cable lengths from shore. Those aboard saw that there were several people on the sea wall, helpless to afford them any asistance. Shortly after eight o'clock a tremendous sea came roaring in toward the ill-fated vessel. Hitting the *Vryheid* with the force of a battering ram, the wave left the ship rocking like a cradle for two or three seconds. Her timbers had been split, and she immediately separated into several sections. About 170 persons found themselves in the sea, and not one of them ever reached land alive. The wreck still held nearly three hundred people who clung fiercely to the various sections that remained above water. The roar of the great billows was soon completely drowned out by the piercing shrieks and cries of the women and the children.

The men now waited for an opportunity to launch the

jolly boat into which they had placed the colonel and eight women, one of whom was his wife. Soon there came a relatively calm period, and the jolly boat was let down into the water. Hardly had the craft pushed away from the side of the wreck than a great wave was seen approaching. It was a towering billow with a breaking crest. Roaring in, it seemed to pause for a moment, and then broke directly into the jolly boat, submerging all nine persons aboard. The boat came to the surface a minute later, bottom up. The colonel could be seen, trying frantically to keep his wife afloat, but another wave rushed in and overwhelmed them. They were not seen again.

Back on the *Vryheid*, conditions went from bad to worse. Without warning a monstrous wave hit the ship, roared along the sloping deck and pulled Captain Scherman's wife and child from his grasp. She was swept across to a stanchion, where she clung, clutching her baby with one hand and the stanchion with the other. The next wave, high and swift, engulfed the two, and when it passed the infant had been torn from her grasp. Caught in the billow, the baby was carried along the deck in knee-deep water and then overboard to death in the sea.

Watching his chances, Captain Scherman reached his wife's side, where he called for several of the crew to help lash her to a chicken coop on which he decided to float ashore with her. The captain was then fastened alongside his wife, after which the coop was cut free from the deck and let overboard with its human cargo.

The couple floated on their makeshift raft for several minutes. It appeared that they were on their way to a safe landing ashore, but then a great fragment of the *Vryheid* disengaged itself from the remainder of the wreck and started ashore. Smashing into the coop, the timbers continued to the beach, but the captain and his wife were drowned.

Still aboard the *Vryheid* were a lieutenant, his wife and two servants of the admiral. When a part of the quarter-galley began to break off, the four persons clambered aboard. A good swimmer, the lieutenant began to kick and guide the galley fragment toward the beach. Just offshore, however, they were engulfed in a great wave, and all drowned.

About this time, the bowsprit was torn off. Many of the women and officers were still clinging to it while a hundred others were in the riggings in various parts of the bow, which was now being driven toward the sea wall by the waves. Those on the stern watched the progress of their companions with utmost interest. Just as the bowsprit appeared to be beyond the reach of danger, a great sea rushed toward shore and broke over it.

The surface of the ocean was soon dotted with the heads of scores of drowning victims. Several men had almost reached the shore, but the backwash of the waves caught and drowned them. A captain of the marines, who was swimming with one hand, was trying to support his wife by the hair of her head. Then came the moment when he was overcome by cold and fatigue. Turning around, he clasped her in his arms and both sank to their death in the sea. Thus perished the last woman aboard the *Vryheid*.

The vessel was gradually disappearing. Many of the seamen and marines leaped into the water in an effort to reach shore, but they soon vanished. By now there were only forty-five people alive on the two parts of the wreck. Each succeeding wave, as the ship kept breaking apart, took one or two of the survivors. Two seamen now decided to lash themselves to a large hog-trough and try to reach the land with its help. They were handed over the larboard * side and, after a miraculous escape from being hit by flying wreckage, actually

* Known today as the port or left side.

succeeded in getting to land safely. They were the first from the *Vryheid* to reach shore alive!

This gave courage to the thirty-three men still aboard the wreck. They began constructing a raft, which when finished was large enough for all of them. They pushed off just as another giant sea struck the *Vryheid* and shattered her into a thousand pieces. The men were now in great peril from the fragments of the wreck which floated about in every direction, but the raft continued to drift toward the sea wall. Suddenly a large piece of the wreck collided with it, drowning seventeen of the thirty-three aboard and injuring many of the others. Starting toward shore again, the raft was caught by a wave ten minutes later and pushed high on the beach.

Half-dead and terribly bruised, the eighteen survivors were hurried to nearby homes, where they were cared for and then put to bed. Thus, of the 472 persons aboard the *Vryheid* only 18 escaped death! Later bodies were found scattered for miles up and down the English coast where they had washed ashore, and were gathered together for interment in a nearby cemetery.

Ironically, a small merchant vessel which left Amsterdam on the same day as the *Vryheid* took a pilot off Margate and was brought back into port without the loss of a single life!

Appendix

LATITUDE AND LONGITUDE OF CRAFT WHICH WENT DOWN IN THE MASSACHUSETTS BAY AREA

42°33′N NATALIE HAMMOND
70°15′W O.C.G.R.

42°30′15″N MORITZ (Am.) C.
70°39′20″W E.S.F.

42°30′N JAMES L. MALLOY
70°42′W O.C.G.R.

42°26′24″N VAN (Am.) C.
70°40′16″W E.S.F.

42°26′04″N GALE (Am.) Tr.
70°37′33″W E.S.F.

42°24′26″N MASSACOIT (Am.) C.
70°39′00″W E.S.F.

42°23′43″N ROMANCE (Am.) P.
70°51′46″W L.H.N. to M. No. 24,
1937

42°23′36″N MIST (Am.) Tr.
70°39′18″W E.S.F.

42°23′19″N OCEAN (Am.) Tr.
70°35′33″W E.S.F.

42°23′N WINIFRED SHERI-
70°55′W DAN
O.C.G.R.

42°22′26″N SALISBURY (Am.)
70°51′35″W E.S.F.

42°22′26″N EAGLE BOAT NO. 42
70°43′23″W E.S.F.

42°22′06″N COYOTE (Am.) C.
70°43′06″W E.S.F.

42°22′03″N KING PHILIP (Am.) P.
70°37′11″W (Small)
E.S.F.

42°20′56″N DREDGE NO. 6 & Tug
70°41′05″W BLUEJAY
E.S.F.

42°20′39″N ROXANA (Am.) Yct.
70°40′43″W E.S.F.

42°20′24″N C. H. SPRAGUE (Am.)
70°40′47″W T.
E.S.F.

42°30′N RESTLESS (Am.) Fh.
70°25′W I ND Ltr. 10 5 42

42°25′05″N HERBERT (Am.)
70°51′25″W I ND Wreck List 9 20 42

42°24′N LEIGH No. 3, (Am.) B
70°50′W I ND Wreck List 9 20 42

42°23′30″N MARY A. WHITE
70°40′25″W (Am.) Sloop
I ND Wreck List 9 20 42

42°23'16"N WRECK
70°51'49"W Salvage operations complete, mass of steel left in above position. Salvage Div. Navy Department

42°09'18"N Pinthis C.
70°33'48"W

42°03'00"N FRANCIS (Am.) Tr.
70°15'39"W

42°28'45"N L. & W. B. C. Co. No. 1
70°45'12"W (Am.) B.
U. S. Engineers, Boston, Mass.

42°23'05"N CORNELIA (Am.) T.
70°45'05"W U. S. Engineers, Boston, Mass.

42°24'30"N CONFIDENCE (Am.) T.
70°39'05"W U. S. Engineers, Boston, Mass.

42°21'50"N VESTA (Am.) T.
70°39'48"W U. S. Engineers, Boston, Mass.

42°21'50"N WILLIAM H. YERKES
70°39'48"W JR. (Am.) T.
U. S. Engineers, Boston, Mass.

42°21'50"N Wreck
70°42'17"W The wreck of a mud scow lies sunk in the listed position. U. S. Engineers, Boston, Mass.

42°21'06"N Wreck
70°42'15"W The wreck of a concrete scow lies sunk in the listed position. U. S. Engineers, Boston, Mass.

42°20'16"N SAM MENGEL (Am.) B.
70°41'00"W U. S. Engineers, Boston, Mass.

42°04'24"N GEORGINA M. (Am.)
70°19'50"W Sch.
U. S. Engineers, Boston, Mass.

42°22'45"N ETHEL N. (Am.) Sch.
70°39'30"W I ND Wreck List 9 20 42

42°22'45"N WAVE (Am.) Tr.
70°39'25"W I ND Wreck List 9 20 42

42°22'24"N JAMES M. HUDSON
70°45'15"W (Am.) B.
I ND Wreck List 9 20 42

42°22'00"N W. A. MARSHALL
70°44'20"W (Am.) B.
I ND Wreck List 9 20 42

42°21'45"N No. 9 (Am.) Dredge
70°41'20"W I ND Wreck List 9 20 42

42°21'45"N JOEL COOK (Am.)
29°40'25"W Lighter
I ND Wreck List 9 20 42

42°21'45"N ANNIE CONANT
(Am.) Lighter

42°21'35"N WRECK (Am.) Lighter
70°39'35"W I ND Wreck List 9 20 42

42°21'25"N BEATRICE (Am.) T.
70°42'15"W I ND Wreck List 9 20 42

42°21'25"N RELIANCE (Am.)
70°42'00"W Lighter
I ND Wreck List 9 20 42

42°21'10"N MC GOWEN (Am.)
70°43'00"W I ND Wreck List 9 20 42
Lighter

42°21'00"N I ND Wreck List 9 20 42
70°42'50"W EVANS (Am.) Lighter

42°16'35"N I ND Wreck List 9 20 42
70°36'26"W SOUTHLAND (Am.) C.

Glossary

The following terms may be of interest to students of the sea:

ABACK When the wind is blowing from ahead and pushing the sail against the mast, that sail is laid aback.

ABAFT In back of or behind.

ABATE To lower in force or intensity.

ABEAM In line at right angles with the ship's length. When a vessel at sea reaches a point of land at her side, that particular location is said to be abeam of her.

ADVENTURER A shareholder in a commercial, privateering, or pirate expedition.

BACKSTAY A long rope or wire leading aft from the upper masthead to the vessel's side or stern, in contrast to a forestay which leads forward.

BEND To attach or fix, to tie, fasten on, or make fast. In ancient days it meant to bring a line into the shape of a bow.

BILGED A vessel's bottom which is staved in. When a craft crashes ashore in this manner she is usually assumed to be beyond repair.

BINNACLE The box holding the compass, located near the helm. It comes from "bittacle," derived from Spanish *bitacula,* "where the compass is kept."

BOWER An anchor with its cable. Each vessel in olden times had its best bower and its small bower at the catheads.

BRIG A square-rigged vessel with two masts.

BROACH To To veer suddenly into the trough of a heavy sea, or to meet the sea.

BULKHEAD One of the upright partitions to separate different parts of the ship.

CATHEAD A beam which projects at each side of the vessel, for raising the anchor or carrying it suspended.

CLEW A lower corner of a square sail, or the aftermost corner of a fore-and-aft sail.

DEADEYE A round laterally flattened wooden block with a groove around it and having three holes bored through it, but no wheel or sheave on which the rope turns, used to receive a lanyard or short piece of rope especially in setting up shrouds.

FLYING JIB A sail set outside the jib sail.

FORESAIL The bottom sail, or course, on the foremast.

FUTTOCK SHROUDS Short shrouds leading from the edge of a fighting top to a point on the mast just below it.

GALIOT A small galley, often without a deck.

GALLEON Origin is Spanish *noa* or *navio*. This large sailing vessel usually had three masts and two or more decks. Ordinarily the galleon had a low waist and a high poop and forecastle. The largest galleons in the Pacific were as large as 1000 tons.

GALLEY Similar to Spanish *galera*. A proportionally long shallow-draft vessel with a single covered deck, propelled by oars and sails. She had speed and maneuverability, but in a storm might capsize.

LUFF To put the helm up and get your craft closer to the wind.

MIZZEN Referring to any part of the aftermost, and shortest, mast of a three-masted sailing ship.

ORLOP Lowest deck in the ship, below the berth deck, containing magazine, stores, etc., and above the hold.

PEAK The upper, outer corner of a four-cornered, fore-and-aft sail.

PINNACE A small ship, light and narrow, propelled by both sail and oars. Ofter it was used as a dispatch boat or tender of a larger ship.

PRIVATEER Ship privately owned and manned but in wartime acting for the government against the enemy. Also a man aboard the same craft.

QUADRANT Graduated piece of metal shaped like a quarter-circle. Used for taking altitudes in navigation.

QUARTER The upper part of a ship's side between the after part of the main chains and the stern. The term was first used in 1599.

RATLINES Small lines fastened across ship's shrouds like ladder rungs.

RUMMAGE To go ashore and ravage the countryside.

SCUTTLE Opening cut in a ship's deck.

SEIZING The fastening together of two ropes by a small rope.

SHEAVE Moving part of a block.

SHEET Rope attached to a sail used to set it and hold it down.

SHIVER To shake the wind out of a sail by bracing it so that the wind blows against the outer edge of it.

SHROUDS A set of ropes or wires, usually in pairs, supporting masts athwartships.

SPANKER After sail of a ship, set fore-and-aft, with a boom and gaff.

SPRITSAIL Sail mounted athwartships on a yard lashed across the bowsprit.

STUDDING SAILS Light sails set outside the principal square sails on specially rigged booms.

TOMPION Wooden plug in the mouth of a gun, originally tampion, serving to exclude rain or sea water.

TOPGALLANT The third sail above the deck on a mast.

TOPMAST The second section of mast above the deck.

TRUNNIONS Projecting bars on a gun barrel which fit into the carriage.

WEARING Turning away from the wind when steering so as to come right round and steer to the other side, with the general object of making progress against a wind blowing from ahead, as in tacking.

WEATHER To sail to the windward of another ship.

YAW To swing off course temporarily. Known as bad steering usually, the expression was first used in 1546 in England.

Index

Addie E. Snow, 57, 58, 61
Addison, Joseph, 197
Admiralty, 200
Aegean Sea, 202
Africa, 3, 154, 164, 169, **172**
Ajax, 202-207
Albany, 18
Alexandria, 101
Allentown, 4
Allerton, Isaac, 32
Alps, 85
Amazon River, 24
Amsterdam, 214-216, 223
Ancient Order of the Hibernians, 42
Andromeda, 80
Anson, Lord, 193
Anson, Mr., 71
Archeologia, 188
Archer, Lt., 80-90
Arctic, 25
Arctic, 121-129
Army's Royal Sappers, 200
Arnold, seaman, 154
Arthur, Chester A., 22
Asapour, 160, 161
Asia, 121, 164, 202
Asiatics, 183, 184
Aspinwall City, 21
Associated Press, 68
Atalante, 91-96

Atkins, Pilot, 10
Atlantic, 91
Atlantic Avenue, 53
Avery family, 32, 33
Avery, his Fall, 35
Avery, Rev. John, 32, 34

Bab, 172
Bahamas, 26
Bailey, Capt. George, 208-210
Bailey Island, Me., 53
Balkan Peninsula, 202
Baltic Sea, 187
Bankhead, Com. John P., **139**, 140
Barasole, 161, 162
Barbadoes, 80
Barrossa, 92
Batavia, 214, 215
Batavian Republic, 214
Bay of Fundy, 25
Bay of St. Helen's, 190
Bay State, 51, 52
Beachey Island, 127
Bearse, Captain, 46, 49
Beaufort, 133
Beaufort, N. C., 130, **139**, 141
Beaver's Prize, 80
Beckholmen, 192
Bengal, 97, 156, 162

Bentang (island), 182, 183
Bickers, Surfman, 56
Biddeford, Me., 9
Billings, Leonard, 17
Bishop, Henry, 196
Black Sea, 202
Blackwood, Capt. Henry, 202-204, 206, 207
Blanchard, Charles, 52
Blanchard, Miss Grace, 52
Blanchard, Capt. Hollis H., 51-53, 55
Bligh, Capt., 183
Block Island, 73-75
Bloomer, Walter, 68
Bombay, 155, 156, 175, 183
Boon Island, 55
Boscawen, Admiral, 193
Bosphorus, 202
Boston, Mass., 3, 6, 7, 22, 32, 37, 40, 43, 49-51, 53, 54, 58-60, 69
Boston Harbor, 3-8, 37-42, 53, 115, 156
Boston Light, 4, 6
Boston Lightship, 3
Bradford, William, 31, 36
Braithwaite and Sons, 199
Brimstone Island, 13
Bristol, Eng., 203
British, 41, 99, 180, 193
British East India Company, 145, 155-158, 162, 170, 174, 198, 214, 215
British State Papers, 189
Brockton, Mass., 53
Brooke, Captain, 163
Brooklin, Me., 60
Brooklyn, N. Y., 131, 134
Brown, Mr., 15
Buchanan, Capt. Franklin, 132, 135
Bulmer, Ian, 191
Burgess Collection of Serpents and Birds, 9
Burt, Captain, 22
Bushnell, Cornelius, 131
Buzzard's Bay, 36

Calcutta, 162, 163
Calcutta Hospital, 163
California, 20
Cambria, 26, 99, 101

Cambridge, Mass., 59
Cameleon, 80
Cameron, Capt. Reuben, 53
Camp Lejeune, N. C., 142
Canada, 118
Canopus, 204
Cape Ann, 32, 35, 55
Cape Cod, 35, 37, 39, 43, 44, 55-59, 61, 62, 65-70, 113, 114, 143
Cape of Good Hope, 147, 165, 170
Cape Hatteras, 19, 139
Cape Hatteras Light, 130, 143
Cape Henry, 139
Cape Henry Light, 134
Cape Horn, 20
Cape Sambro, 91
Cape Sambro Light, 91, 92
Carewe, Sir Gawen, 188
Carewe, Sir George, 188, 189
Carewe, Sir Peter, 188, 189
Caroline, 101, 102
Carver, Capt. Charles G., 61, 62
Castine, Me., 11
Cattack, 161, 162
Central America, 19-28
Charles, Duke of Suffolk, 189
Charlestown, Mass., 131
Charlestown Navy Yard, 131
Chase, Surfman, 66
Chatham, Mass., 65, 68
Chelsea, Mass., 2
Chestnut Street (Chelsea), 37
China, 97, 175, 177, 183
Chinese Ocean, 175-184
City of Columbus, 43-49
City of Salisbury, 4, 7, 8
Civil War, 130-143
Coast Guard, 8
Cobb, Capt. Henry, 97, 98, 101
Coen, General, 214
Cohasset, Mass., 38-42, 55
Cohasset Rocks, 42
Collins, Edward K., 113-120
Collins, Capt. John, 113
Collins Line, 25, 113
Colon, 21
Colorados Roads, 103
Conflans, 193
Congress, 133

Cook, Captain, 101
Coombs family, 13
Coombs, Roy, 13
Coote, Col., 162
Cordilleras, 87
Cork, 208
Cornish, 99
Coromandel, 163
Cowper, William, 200
Craney Island, 135, 139
Cremona, 94
Crescent City, 26
Crozier, Francis, 121
Cuba, 21, 81, 83, 86, 89, 90, 102
Cumberland, 133
Currituck, 134
Cuttyhunk Island, 46

D'Estaung, Count, 156
Dardanelles, 202
David (Psalmist), 15
Davidson, Lt., 135
Dawson, Mr., 26
Deal, 217, 218
Deal Castle, 80
Deal Harbor, 218
Dealy Island, 128
Deer Island, 7
Delagos Bay, 173
Dennison, Capt. Alexander, 51, 52
Devil's Back, 45
Devil's Bridge, 45, 46, 49
Dexter, 47
Dexter's Locomotive Museum, 9
Doddington, 147-155
Dover, 217, 218
Dramatic line, 113
Duckworth, Admiral John, 202
Dundas, Capt., 170
Durham, Lt., 195
Dutch, 214, 215
Dutch East India Company, 164, 165, 169, 173
Dutchman, 165
Dyer, Captain, 15, 16
Dymchurch, 219
Dymchurch Wall, 217, 218

Eames, Thomas Harrison, 57
East India Company (British), 147, 155-158, 162, 170, 174, 198, 214, 215
East India Company (Dutch), 164, 165, 169, 173
East India Roadstead, 165
East Indies, 81, 214
Eastern Point, Mass., 54
Eastport, Me., 17
Eastport Harbor, 10
Edgar Randall, 54
El Dorado, 23
Eldridge, Captain, 66, 67
Eliot, William, 32
Elizabeth and Ann, 4
Elizabeth River, 133, 135
Ellen, 24, 25
Ellis, surfman, 65, 66, 68, 69
Elphinstone, 175
Endeavor, 80
England, 9, 32, 97, 99, 101, 114, 116, 118, 121, 122, 129, 147, 156, 159, 161-163, 173, 174, 187-191, 194-201, 208, 217
English Navy, 188, 197
Enterprise (H.M.S.), 122
Erebus, 121
Ericsson, Capt. John, 130-132, 141
Eskimos, 123
Europe, 3, 121, 202
Europeans, 161, 177, 181, 182, 184
Ewan Crewar, 4
Exile, 4

Fall River, Mass., 25
Falmouth, Eng., 101
Fanny, 175-184
Fattysalam, 156-159, 163
Favorite, 115
Fisher, Samuel O., 55, 56
Fitzpatrick, 65, 67
Florence E. Stream, 54
Forbes, Robert Bennet, 44, 49
Foye, surfman, 66
Fox Island Thoroughfare, 10-18
France, 152
Franklin, Sir John, 121, 126-129
Franklin Expedition, 123, 127

Franzen, Anders, 191
French, 156-163, 173, 188, 189, 193, 197
Fuller, Edwin, 44
Fuller, H. H., 13, 14

Galway Ireland, 36
Ganges River, 160, 161, 163
Garnet, 114
Garrick, 113, 114
Gate City, 45
Gay Head Indians, 46, 47
Gay Head Lighthouse, 46
George, Mr., 24-27
George Al, 61-64
George the First, 197
George Law, 19
Georgia, 49, 80
Glades, 39
Glades House, 38
Glasgow, 115
Glaucus, 46, 49
Gloucester, Mass., 31, 53, 54
Good Hope, 147
Goodinoh, Mr., 84
Gordon, Major, 157
Gott, George, 60, 61
Grampus, 38
Grant, Alexander, 25
Graves Ledge, 4
Grayling, 53, 54
Great Gales and Dire Disasters, 91
Great Lakes, 51
Greate Henry, 188
Greene, Lt., 137
Greenland, 121
Greenock, Scotland, 118
Greenpoint, 131
Griswald, John A., 131
Gulf of Mexico, 50, 103-108
Gulf of Tonkin, 177

Hainan, 177, 184
Haley, Frank T., 75
Half Way House, 56
Halifax, N. S., 92, 96
Halifax Harbor, 91, 92

Halstead, Sir Laurence, 107, 108
Hampton Roads, 133-135, 138, 139
Hansen, Marie, 59, 60
Happy Deliverance, 153
Harry Knowlton, 71, 75
Hathaway, Capt. Lynes B., 53
Havana, Cuba, 21, 89
Hawk, 163
Hazard, 4
Heirgsell, Fred, 74
Herbert, John R., 192
Herndon, Ellen, 21, 22
Herndon, Capt. W. L., 21-24, 27
Hesperus, 115
Hickey, Capt. Frederick, 91-95
Highland Light, 59, 61, 62
Hispaniola, 19
Holdernesse, 163
Holland, 164, 165, 169
Holland, Corporal, 142
Horse Island, 165
House of Commons, 122
Howard, Pilot S. P., 134
Howe, Lord, 193
Humane Societies of London and Liverpool, 114
Hyannis, Mass., 58
Hybertsson, Heinrich, 190
Hythe, 217
Hythe Bay, 217

India, 156, 160-162, 170, 175
India Wharf, 51, 59
Indian Seas, 156
Indiana encampment, 142
Indians, 155
Indochina, 177
Intrepid, 129
Investigator, 122, 126-128
Ipswich, Mass., 32
Ireland, 36, 161
Irish, 37-42
Isle au Haut, 16, 17
Isthmus of Panama, 20, 21

Jamaica, 79, 81, 89, 107
Jamestown, 135

Janus, 90
Java, 214, 215
Jeans, Capt. John, 117, 118
Jeffers, Capt., 138
Jersey, 197
Jesus of Lubich, 190
Joachim, 4
Johnson, Surfman John, 56, 57
Jones, Richard P., 200
Jones, Capt. Thomas ap Catesby, 135-137
Jonge Thomas, 164-167, 169
Joy Line, 70

Kadosh, 4
Kastellholmen, 192
Kathleen, 38, 39
Kearney, Captain, 156-163
Kellett, Captain, 128
Kelly, Jim, 57
Kempenfelt, Lt. Colonel, 197
Kempenfelt, Gustavus Adolphus, 197
Kempenfelt, Adm. Richard, 196, 197, 199, 201
Kendrick, surfman, 66, 67
Kent, 216
Kent, 97-102
Killarney, 208-213
King Gustaf V, drydock, 192
King Henry VIII, 188, 189, 199
King James the Second, 197
King's Yard, 199
Knowlton, 71, 75
Kohler, F. D., 20
Kohler Ingot, 20

La Blanche, 80
Lancaster Sound, 121
Larchmont, 70-75
Lascars, 160-162, 179, 181-184
Laurel, 80
Law, 19
Lawe, Mrs., 210
Lawke, 193
Leo (dog), 73
Lewis, Capt. William H., 8
Light, John, 143

Lighthouse Dept., 53
Lincoln, President Abraham, 138, 139
Liscomb, John, 51
Lisle, John Viscount, 190
Little, Thomas, 200
Littlefield, Addie, 74
Littlefield, Elam P., 73, 74
Liverpool, Eng., 101, 116, 118
Logoa Bay, 155
London, Eng., 163, 200
Londoner Ledge, 53, 55
Long Island, Mass., 156
Long Island Sound, 72
Longfellow, Henry Wadsworth, 115

MacDonald, Roderick A., 44, 48
Mackenzie River, 127
Mackey, Robert, 7
MacLean, Jack, 108-112
MacNeill, Ben Dixon, 142
Madagascar, 155, 173
Madden, Dr. R. R., 115, 119, 120
Madras, 155, 156, 173, 174
Magpie, 102
Mahrattas, 162
Maine, 9-19, 50-54, 60, 61, 75, 115
Malacca, 181-184
Malay, 182, 183
Malden, Mass., 61
Mallows, Captain, 68
Manby, Captain, 213
Marblehead, Mass., 32, 35
Margate, 223
Marine, 22, 23, 26
Marines, (2nd), 142
Maritana, 4
Marjoram, William, 15, 16
Marshall, Engineer, 10
Martha Bray, 89
Martha's Vineyard, 43-45
Marx, Robert, 142, 143
Mary, 26
Mary Rose, 187-190, 199
Massachusetts, 3-5, 25, 31-65, 79, 113, 131, 156, 192
Massachusetts Bay, 6
Massachusetts Humane Society, 68
Maud S., 53

Mauritius, 173
Maury. Com. Matthew Fontaine, 21
Maynard, Nelson, 7
Mayo, Capt. Elmer, 65, 68, 69
McClintock, Capt. Francis, 129
McClure, Sir Robert, 123, 126
McMullen, Raynor T., 142
McVey, Capt. G. W., 71, 72, 74
Medford, Mass., 8, 59
Meldrum, Tom, 108-112
Melville Castle, 214
Menemsha Bight, 44, 48
Merrimac, 130-139, 141
Mexican War, 24
Mexico, 24
Minerva, 183
Minnesota, 133, 135-138
Minot's Ledge, 37
Minot's Ledge Lighthouse, 38, 55
Mogul, the elephant, 10, 12, 13
Monitor, 130-143
Monomoy, 65-69
Monomoy Lifesaving Crew, 65
Monomoy Point, 65
Montague, 198
Montego Bay, 89, 90
Monticello, 55, 58
Morris, Capt. Owen, 7
Morro Castle, 21
Morton, Capt. Thomas, 5, 6
Motherbank, 198
Mozambique Channel, 170, 172, 173
Mutiny on the Bounty, 183
Mysteries and Adventures Along the Atlantic Coast, 115

Natal, 154
Naushon, 48
Nelson, Lord, 80
Nelson, Mrs., 162
Netherlands, 214
New Brunswick, 9, 16, 17
New England, 29-75, 114
New Sarum, 32
New Shoreham Lifesaving Station, 73, 74
New York, 12, 50-52, 80, 118, 119, 130, 131, 134

Newbury, Mass., 32
Nickerson, surfman, 66
Nickerson's Wharf, 43
Norfolk, Va., 137, 139
Norfolk Navy Yard, 137
North Carolina, 19, 27, 130, 139, 141, 142
North Star, 127, 129
Northern Avenue Bridge, 43
Northwest Passage, 121, 123, 126, 127
Norwegian, 24
Nova Scotia, 55, 58, 91, 92, 96

Old State House, 60
Oliver, Captain, 38
"On the Loss of the *Royal George*," 201
Outer Beach, 58
Ordnance Dept., 137

Paarden, 165
Page, Second Mate, 175-177, 179, 180, 182, 183
Paget, Sir William, 189, 190
Panama, 20, 21
Paracels, 178
Parker, Sir Hyde, 80, 81, 83, 85, 86, 89, 90
Pasley, Col. Charles, 200
Passaic, 139
Patrick Henry, 135
Patriot Ledger, 192
Patten, Stimson, 16
Peaked Hill Bar Buoy, 62
Peaked Hill Bar Station, 56
Peaks of Teneriffe, 83
Pease, Horace N., 46, 47
Peckell, Andreas, 191
Pellier, Capt. D. J., 54
Penobscot Bay, 9, 10, 13
Pennsylvania, 50
Pennsylvania, 180
Pentagoet, 57, 58
Peter Smith, 65
Philadelphia, Pa., 50
Phillip, Sir Thomas, 188
Phipps, Sir William, 19

Phoenix, 79-90
Pilgrim Monument, 62
Pilgrims, 31, 79
Pim, Lt., 128
Piscataqua, 32
Plassy, 162
Plimoth Plantation, 36
Plover, 123
Plymouth, Mass., 79
Point Barrow, 123
Point Shirley, Mass., 7
Polar Seas, 128
Pondicherry, 156
Poole, Frederick, 46
Porcupine, 89, 90
Port Antonio, 80
Port Royal, 80, 90
Portland, 50-64
Portland, Me., 10, 17, 50-52, 54
Portland Associates, 59
Portland Harbor, 52
Portland Steam Packet Company, 51, 61
Portland storm, 70
Portobello, 197
Portsea, 199
Portsmouth Dock-yard, 198
Portsmouth, Eng., 188, 197-199
Portsmouth, N. H., 55
Portuguese, 172, 180
Portuguese Cove, 96
Prescott, George Luther, 60
Prince Albert, 126
Providence, R. I., 36, 70, 74
Provincetown, Mass., 58
Pulo Tingey (island), 182
Puritans, 31

Quebec, 115, 118
Queen Anne, 197
Quincy, Mass., 4, 5, 192

Race Point Coast Guard Station, 55-57, 62
Race Point Life Saving Station, 55-57, 62
Rajah of Asapour, 160, 161

Rajah of Cattack, 161
Raleigh, 133
Ramsey, Engineer, 137
Randall, 54
Reed, Capt. Thomas, 11-13, 15-17
Regavlas, 62
Resolute, 126, 128, 129
Rhode Island, 36, 70, 74
Rhode Island, 139, 140
Rhodes, Lieutenant, 47
Richmond, Va., 139
Roanoke, 133
Robertson, Captain, 175-180
Rockland, Me., 61, 62, 75
Rockport, Mass., 55
Rodney, Lord, 193
Rogers, surfman, 66, 67
Roscius, 113-115, 117-120
Rose, 155
Rowles, George, 208
Royal George, 187, 193-201
Royal Navy, 80
Royal Swedish Navy, 191
Royal Tar, 9-18
Royal United Service Institution, 200
Russell, Lord, 189
Ryan, Mr., 49

Sabine Point, 71
Sachem, 134
Sacramento Ingots, 20
St. George, 205
Saint John, 37-42
Saint John, N. B., 9-11, 16, 17
Saint Lawrence, 133
St. Lucia, 154
Salisbury, 4, 7, 8
Salisbury Pinnacle, 8
Sambro Island, 22
Sambro Light, 91, 92
Sampson, 190
Sampson, Captain, 147
San Francisco, Cal., 20
Sandy Point, 73
Sandy Point Lighthouse, 73
Satovan, William J., 8
Saunders, Bruce, 198
Savannah, Ga., 49, 80

Savannah-la-Mar, 79
Savannah Line, 43
Scanty, Hendrick, 150
Scarborough, 80
Sherman, Captain, 215, 219
Scherman, Mrs., 216, 217, 221
Scituate, Mass., 38
Scorpion, 174
Scotia, 114-119
Scotland, 117
Scott, officer, 159
Scripture, Capt. Frank, 55
Sea of Marmara, 202
Senna, 173
Sentry, Captain, 197
Seth Low, 134
Sewall's Point, 138
Shag Rocks, 4, 6
Shakespeare, 113, 114
Shanks, Samuel, 95, 96
Sheridan, 113, 114
Shirley Street (Winthrop), 5
Shovelful Shoal, 65
Siddons, 113-115
Siebe, Augustus, 200
Sister's Rocks, 92
Smith, 65
Smith, Lt. Edward, 103-108
Snow, 57, 58, 61
Snow, Anna-Myrle, 142
Snow, Lt. Edward Rowe, 62
Snow family, 18
Snow, John I., 75
Snow, Willis, 18
Sofala, 172, 173
Soleil Royale, 193
Sonora, 20
Sons and Daughters of the Portland
    Associates, 59
South Africa, 165
South America, 20
South Boston, 43
Sow and Pigs Lightship, 48
Spanish, 19
Spectator, 197
Spithead, 188, 189, 197-200
Squibnocket, 47
Staples, Quartermaster, 71, 72
State of Georgia, 139

Sterling Castle, 80
Stockholm Harbor, 190-193
Stone, Captain, 23
Stone, Henry, 122, 123
Straits of Malacca, 182
*Strange Tales from Nova Scotia to
    Cape Hatteras,* 141
Stream, 54
Stream, Frank, 54
Suffolk, Charles, Duke of, 189, 190
Superbe, 193
Swan Song of Parson Avery, 35
Swan, William U., 55, 68
Swaney family, 39, 42
Swaney, Patrick, 39, 42
Sweden, 150, 187, 190-193, 197

Taite, Mrs., 161, 162
Tarpaulan Cove, 44
Tarpaulin Light, 48
Tarr, Capt. A. A., 53
Tedesco, 4
Tenedos, 205, 206
Terrace Avenue (Winthrop), 5
Terror, 121
Thacher, Mrs., 33-35
Thacher, Anthony, 31-35
Thacher family, 32, 33, 35
Thacher, Mary, 34
Thacher, Peter, 32
Thacher, William, 34
Thacher's Island, 31, 53-55
Thacher's Island Light, 53
Thacher's Woe, 35
Thames, 122
Thomas, 164-167, 169
Thomas, William, 53
Thompson, Mate, 99
Thoreau, Henry David, 39, 40
Thornquist, John A., 59
Thunderer, 80
Tice, Mr., 26
Timby, Theodore R., 132
Tobago, 90
Treasure, 3-28
Treileben, Hans von, 191
Tremont Theatre, 69
Triangle Ledges, 18

True Tales of Buried Treasure, 19
Truro, Mass., 113, 114
Tulliar, 172
Tyler, Edwin B., 57

Union Navy, 133-144
United States Navy, 21, 130-143
Universalist Church, 37
Ushant, 197

Van Rennselaer, Chief Officer, 23
Vansittart, Mr., 162, 163
Vasa, 187, 190-194
Vasa Committee, 191
Vasa Dockyard, 192
Vasa Museum, 192
Vasavarset, 192, 193
Venetian, 189
Vera Cruz, 99
Vernon, 4
Veto, 11, 12, 15, 16
Victor, 80
Victory, 200
Vinalhaven, Me., 9, 13
Vineyard Sound, 44
Virginia, 139
Virginia, 131
von Treileben, Hans, 191
Vryheid, 214-223

Wadena, 65, 66
Waghorne, Captain, 196, 197
War of 1812, 114
Ward, Captain, 162
Warspite, 197
Washington, D. C., 6, 139, 141
Washington Naval Observatory, 24
Watch Hill Light, 71
Watch and Wait, 31-36

Weekahaug Lifesaving Station, 75
Welsh, 135
West Indies, 79
Westminster, 197
Whidah, 143
White, Captain, 163
Whitehead, 42
Whittier, John Greenleaf, 35
William IV of Eng., 9
Williams, Captain, 91
Willoughby, Lt. Nisbit, 205, 206
Wiltshire, Eng., 32
Winslow, John F., 131
Winterton, 170-174
Winthrop, Mass., 4
Winthrop, Dean, 4, 5
Winthrop, John, 4
Wiscasset, Me., 115
Wise, Capt. H. A., 137
Wollaston, Mass., 8
Woltemad, 169
Woltemad, Corporal, 166, 169
Woltemad, Zookeeper, 165-167, 169
Women of the Sea, 113
Wood, Charles, 5
Wood, Lieutenant, 202, 203
Wooden, carpenter, 82
Woolwich, 193
Worden, Capt. John Lorimer, 132, 134-138
Wreck of the Hesperus, 115
Wright, Capt. S. C., 44, 45, 49
Wyman, Mr., 71, 72

Yarmouth, Mass., 35
Young, Purser, 73
Young, Mrs. Anna, 60
Young, Cy, 58

"Zoo Ship," 4, 7, 8